Russian Military Strategy

Organizing Operations for the Initial Period of War

CLINT REACH, ALEXIS A. BLANC, EDWARD GEIST

Prepared for the United States European Command
Approved for public release; distribution unlimited

NATIONAL SECURITY RESEARCH DIVISION

For more information on this publication, visit **www.rand.org/t/RRA1233-1**

About RAND

The RAND Corporation is a research organization that develops solutions to public policy challenges to help make communities throughout the world safer and more secure, healthier and more prosperous. RAND is nonprofit, nonpartisan, and committed to the public interest. To learn more about RAND, visit www.rand.org.

Research Integrity

Our mission to help improve policy and decisionmaking through research and analysis is enabled through our core values of quality and objectivity and our unwavering commitment to the highest level of integrity and ethical behavior. To help ensure our research and analysis are rigorous, objective, and nonpartisan, we subject our research publications to a robust and exacting quality-assurance process; avoid both the appearance and reality of financial and other conflicts of interest through staff training, project screening, and a policy of mandatory disclosure; and pursue transparency in our research engagements through our commitment to the open publication of our research findings and recommendations, disclosure of the source of funding of published research, and policies to ensure intellectual independence. For more information, visit www.rand.org/about/research-integrity.

RAND's publications do not necessarily reflect the opinions of its research clients and sponsors.

Published by the RAND Corporation, Santa Monica, Calif.
© 2022 RAND Corporation
RAND® is a registered trademark.

Library of Congress Cataloging-in-Publication Data is available for this publication.
ISBN: 978-1-9774-0712-2

Cover: Fedor Leukhin.

About This Report

This report is part of ongoing research on Russian military assessments and planning.[1] A previous study showed that in overall military potential—a broad measure including political, economic, and military indicators—Russia perceives itself as the weaker power in the confrontation with the United States and the North Atlantic Treaty Organization (NATO). This contrasts with Western assessments focused on Russia's military advantages along its western periphery. The contradictory dynamics of Russian local superiority and overall inferiority led to the research questions of this report: How is Russia developing its military strategy to mitigate perceived weakness? In a period of crisis, is Russia preparing to exploit local advantages to strike the lightning blow and win the decisive battle? Or is it building an armed force based on defensive operational concepts to exhaust NATO of its advantages in the initial period of war?

In this report, we examine several factors to assess the orientation of Russian military strategy. These factors include the balance of power, Russian diplomacy with China, views on the character of future war, and trends in force readiness and mobilization. We also explore existing operational concepts to understand how Russia is planning to execute its military strategy.

RAND National Security Research Division

This publication was funded by the Russia Strategic Initiative, United States European Command, and conducted within the International Security and Defense Policy Center of the RAND National Security Research Division (NSRD), which operates the RAND National Defense Research Institute (NDRI), a federally funded research and development center sponsored by the Office of the Secretary of Defense, the Joint Staff, the Unified Combat-

[1] Clint Reach, Alyssa Demus, Eugeniu Han, Bilyana Lilly, Krystyna Marcinek, Yuliya Shokh, *Russian Military Forecasting and Analysis: The Military-Political Situation and Military Potential in Strategic Planning*, Santa Monica, Calif.: RAND Corporation, RR-A198-4, 2022.

ant Commands, the Navy, the Marine Corps, the defense agencies, and the defense intelligence enterprise.

For more information on the RAND International Security and Defense Policy Center, see www.rand.org/nsrd/isdp or contact the director (contact information is provided on the webpage).

Summary

The research for this report was conducted in 2021, prior to Russia's invasion of Ukraine in February 2022.

From Moscow's perspective, the global military-political situation is evolving in a way that makes a great power war with the North Atlantic Treaty Organization (NATO)—an economically and technologically superior alliance—the most likely large-scale scenario for which the Russian military must prepare. How is Russia developing its military strategy from a position of overall weakness? Russia might pursue attrition of the stronger power to exhaust the enemy of its advantages. Or it could attack aggressively in the initial period of war to avoid decisive defeat. Given numerous references at the most senior levels of the Russian military to Aleksandr Svechin, a Soviet strategist who advocated strategic defense against the "capitalist countries" in the 1920s, perhaps Russia might be oriented to the former.

After exploring a number of factors to assess the orientation of Russian military strategy, we found little evidence that Russia is prioritizing attrition and defense in the initial period of war. Given Russia's perceived weakness relative to NATO, we expected Russian officers to consider historical precedent in which the weaker side has embraced defensive concepts to reduce the advantages of an economically and technologically superior opponent in war.

In fact, Russian operational planning for the initial period of war is geared toward preemption and destruction with ready forces based on a set of assumptions about NATO actions. The most important Russian assumption is that NATO is in the process of building up sufficient forces to credibly launch an attack against Russia. Because Russia believes that NATO, in this scenario, could generate decisive effects at the outset of the war through conventional long-range strikes deep into Russian territory, it does not prioritize strategic defensive actions. If war is inevitable, Russia believes that it must attack NATO at the outset and focus on functional destruction of key targets (see Figures S.1 and S.2) through coordinated or simultaneous strategic operations.

Russia's emphasis in the initial period is on the employment of "all available forces and means" to reduce NATO's ability to conduct an aerospace

FIGURE S.1

Example of Russian View on Character of Future War into the 2030s

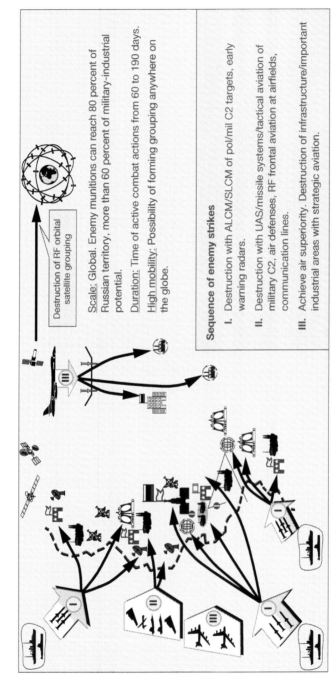

Destruction of RF orbital satellite grouping

Scale: Global. Enemy munitions can reach 80 percent of Russian territory, more than 60 percent of military-industrial potential.

Duration: Time of active combat actions from 60 to 190 days.

High mobility: Possibility of forming grouping anywhere on the globe.

Sequence of enemy strikes

I. Destruction with ALCM/SLCM of pol/mil C2 targets, early warning radars.

II. Destruction with UAS/missile systems/tactical aviation of military C2, air defenses, RF frontal aviation at airfields, communication lines.

III. Achieve air superiority. Destruction of infrastructure/important industrial areas with strategic aviation.

SOURCE: V. M. Burenok, "Razvitie systemy vooruzheniia i novyi oblik Vooruzhennykh sil RF," *Zaschita i bezopasnost'*, No. 2, 2009.
NOTE: ALCM = air-launched cruise missile; C2 = command and control; pol/mil = political/military; RF = Russian Federation; SLCM = submarine-launched cruise missile; UAS = unmanned aerial system. Image reproduced courtesy of East View Information Services.

FIGURE S.2

Potential Russian Actions in Future Great Power War in the 2030s

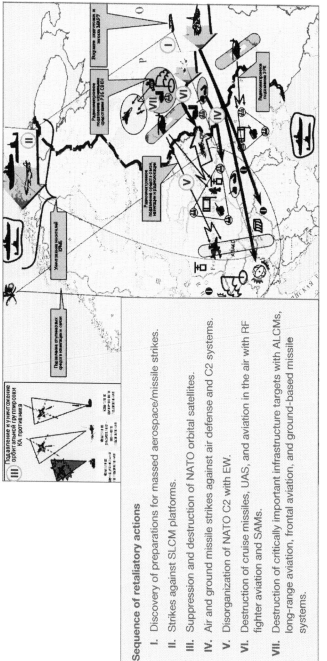

Sequence of retaliatory actions

I. Discovery of preparations for massed aerospace/missile strikes.

II. Strikes against SLCM platforms.

III. Suppression and destruction of NATO orbital satellites.

IV. Air and ground missile strikes against air defense and C2 systems.

V. Disorganization of NATO C2 with EW.

VI. Destruction of cruise missiles, UAS, and aviation in the air with RF fighter aviation and SAMs.

VII. Destruction of critically important infrastructure targets with ALCMs, long-range aviation, frontal aviation, and ground-based missile systems.

SOURCE: Burenok, 2009.

NOTES: EW = electronic warfare; SAM = surface-to-air missile. Image reproduced courtesy of East View Services.

attack against Russian territory or military forces. A related course of action is to use superior, ready ground forces to impose a contact war on NATO. Sufficient destruction of the aerospace system is crucial from Russia's perspective, however, because gains on the ground could be fleeting if Russia is not able to deny air superiority and disrupt NATO force flows from the United States and across the European continent. This dynamic shifts the focus away from Russian ground forces toward Russian capacity to conduct sustained theater strikes, a relative weakness in Russian military potential.

The influence of this weakness is found in Russia's leading principles of warfare and recent operational innovations. In particular, the contradiction between Russia's destructive mindset and its economic constraints have led to a focus on asymmetric targeting of military and nonmilitary infrastructure—a so-called indirect approach focused on functional destruction of the attacking military and military-economic potential of any society supporting the war. First, this means a gradual shift from destroying forward troop groupings toward prioritizing the destruction of command, control, communications, computers, intelligence, surveillance, and reconnaissance (C4ISR) and other critical infrastructure that supports the NATO aerospace attack system. Second, around 2008, Russia developed a strategic operation whose primary objective is to conventionally destroy military-industrial capacity and the infrastructure that supports life in NATO countries. One objective of the latter action is to instill panic in target populations and reduce their will to fight. Russia appears to judge that this escalatory action is worth the risk, because less-decisive action could lead to rapid defeat or a prolonged war that Russia might struggle to win if the war remained conventional. In brief, Russian planning suggests an initial course of action closer to total war than limited war.

Russian focus on indirect or asymmetric approaches to warfare is not unlike the Air War Plans Division-1 of the late 1930s, which sought to rapidly destroy German air bases, electric power plants, transportation networks, oil refineries, aluminum plants, and other critical infrastructure without which planners assumed that it would be impossible to continue the war. Back then, the lack of true precision and range left the plan mostly ineffective in the actual war. Russia is developing the precision and range required to attempt a similar plan in modern conditions, although challenges remain.

Challenges in Russian Execution of Military Strategy

The overall contours of Russian military strategy are relatively apparent. Future research will need to address Russia's ability to execute operational concepts. Although only briefly alluded to in this report, our research revealed at least two areas that could challenge Russia's execution in wartime. These include munitions capacity and C2. In regard to the former, in military conflicts since 1991, the destruction of military and nonmilitary targets through precision strike has been a resource-intensive effort. This would likely be even more true in a high-intensity conflict in Europe, where there is an abundance of targets. According to General Valerii Gerasimov, the chief of Russia's General Staff, Russia nevertheless intends to continue to build out its long-range precision strike complex to the extent that these weapons will one day largely replace nonstrategic nuclear weapons in Russia's strategic deterrence framework. Reducing reliance on nonstrategic nuclear weapons would allow Russia to "lengthen the bridge" between conventional and nuclear war in a future great power conflict. However, the quantitative requirements for long-range conventional weapons, particularly in the face of future NATO countermeasures, could be quite high.

Strategic operations, based on historical precedent, are those that require the C2 of multiple joint strategic commands (JSCs). Russia does not intend for JSC West alone to fight NATO. JSC North, South, and Center at a minimum will likely be involved at or near the outset of hostilities. Preliminarily, we can say that the C2 of a large, joint force has been and continues to be a challenge in Russian military art. The creation and maintenance of reliable lines of communication to issue directives, share battlefield information, and coordinate actions between the JSCs is a complex technical requirement for Russia to conduct the type of operations discussed above, which, according to one analyst, had not been satisfactorily resolved as of a few years ago. To address the challenges of coordination and allocation of forces and means in joint, large-scale operations, Russia is in the process of consolidating its strategic operational concepts. SODCIT has reportedly been merged with the strategic operation of nuclear forces to ensure "efficient allocation of enemy targets between nuclear forces and forces equipped with strategic nonnuclear weapons [and to] facilitate joint planning and employment of nuclear and strategic nonnuclear forces in a coordinated plan under the Supreme Commander-in-Chief and under direct control of the Russian

General Staff."[1] In 2019, a General-Major from the Main Operations Directorate of the General Staff suggested that further consolidation of strategic operations was likely.

A final question regarding Russian military strategy is found in the underlying assumption of the decisive end to a war in which each side possesses large amounts of material and human resources. The overall power imbalance is significantly in favor of the West, to be sure. But Russia has a large military, population, and territory. It would be a departure from most of the history of great power wars for such a conflict to be concluded in a matter of weeks or a few months. If the long-range strike campaign of both sides in the initial period proves less decisive than anticipated, and if the war were to remain conventional—arguably the only way in which fighting the war would make political sense—then there is the possibility of a protracted war. Despite much of the evidence pointing to Russia staking its military strategy on destruction in the initial period, recent efforts to more closely engage China diplomatically and build a more effective Russian state mobilization system suggest that Moscow may be hedging against this protracted contingency.

---

[1] V. G. Ivanov, A. Iu. Savitskii, and S. G. Makarov, "Vliianie voin i vooruzhennykh konfliktov na sistemu sviazi voennogo naznacheniia," in *Radiolokatsiia, navigatsiia, sviaz': Sbornik trudov XXVI Mezhdunarodnoi nauchno-tekhnicheskoi konferentsii*, Tom 2, Voronezhskii gosudarstvennoi universitet / Sozvezdie Contsern, 2020, p. 248.

Contents

Figures and Tables

Figures

Tables

CHAPTER ONE

Introduction

The research for this report was conducted in 2021, prior to Russia's invasion of Ukraine in February 2022.

Beginning in the late 1960s, a rough balance of power set the conditions for Soviet military strategy. As of 2020, the overall power dynamics are exceedingly working against Russia from the perspectives of state power and military potential.[1] At virtually no point in the past four centuries has the European continent been so aligned politically and militarily, and China has surpassed Russia in several state power indicators.[2] Russia nevertheless has defined its national interests in terms of resisting the U.S.-backed European integration system, challenging or supplanting U.S. influence around the globe, and pursuing an "independent foreign policy" that could bring it into conflict with China at some point in the future. Russian words and deeds have shown that its military power is a key element to the confrontation.

But the orientation of Russian military strategy vis-à-vis the North Atlantic Treaty Organization (NATO) is not immediately obvious, particularly given the contradictory dynamics of local military superiority and overall inferiority. Wargames and analysis in the United States and elsewhere in

---

[1] Clint Reach, Alyssa Demus, Eugeniu Han, Bilyana Lilly, Krystyna Marcinek, and Yuliya Shokh, *Russian Military Forecasting and Analysis: The Military-Political Situation and Military Potential in Strategic Planning*, Santa Monica, Calif.: RAND Corporation, RR-A198-4, 2022.

[2] We make this assessment on European alignment because 27 European countries in the European Union and 28 countries in Europe are members of NATO, along with the United States and Canada. We are not aware of there ever being such a large portion of Europe in standing political and military alliances. The addition of the United States and Canada tips the scales even further.

the West have repeatedly shown that Russia has consequential advantages on the ground and can pose a serious challenge to NATO airpower with its integrated air defense system in its western strategic direction.[3] Other commentary has emphasized the power imbalance between NATO and Russia and downplayed the Russian threat.[4] This situation, complicated further by Russia's nuclear arsenal, has led to different interpretations—e.g., an aggressive Russia willing to bet on "decisive battle," and a defensive Russia—each of which has different implications for U.S. and NATO counterstrategy.[5] In this report, we assess how Russia is developing its military strategy and operations for regional or large-scale war from a position of overall weakness.

Historical and contemporary analysis of strategy for the initial period of great power war has tended to focus on two concepts—destruction (or decisive battle) and attrition.[6] *Destruction* prioritizes offensive actions in the initial period of war to decisively defeat the opponent on the battlefield in a matter of weeks or months to achieve a political objective. *Attrition* in Russian texts often emphasizes initial defense to exhaust an opponent of advantages and "winning a number of small successes in order to combine them in the long run into a general overall victory."[7]

---

[3] David Ochmanek, Peter A. Wilson, Brenna Allen, Speed Meyers, and Carter C. Price, *U.S. Military Capabilities and Forces for a Dangerous World*, Santa Monica, Calif.: RAND Corporation, RR-1782-1-RC, 2017, pp. 31–47; David A. Shlapak, *The Russian Challenge*, Santa Monica, Calif.: RAND Corporation, PE-250-A, 2018; and Eva Hagström Frisell and Krister Pallin, eds., *Western Military Capability in Northern Europe 2020*, Part I: *Collective Defence*, Stockholm: Swedish Defence Research Agency, FOI-R--5012--SE, February 2021.

[4] James Dobbins, Howard J. Shatz, and Ali Wyne, *Russia Is a Rogue, Not a Peer; China Is a Peer, Not a Rogue: Different Challenges, Different Responses*, Santa Monica, Calif.: RAND Corporation, PE-310-A, 2019; Barry R. Posen, "Europe Can Defend Itself," *Survival*, Vol. 62, No. 6, December 2020–January 2021; and Joshua Shifrinson, "Russia: A Problem, Not a Threat," *Newsweek*, April 21, 2021.

[5] Charles Dick, *Russian Ground Forces: Posture Towards the West*, London: Chatham House, Royal Institute of International Affairs, April 2019, p. 5.

[6] Cathal J. Nolan, *The Allure of Battle: A History of How Wars Have Been Won and Lost*, New York: Oxford University Press, 2017.

[7] A. A. Kokoshin and V. V. Larionov, "Origins of the Intellectual Rehabilitation of A. A. Svechin," in Aleksandr A. Svechin, *Strategy*, Kent D. Lee, ed., Minneapolis, Minn.: East View Publications, 1991, p. 8.

Destruction and attrition historically have been closely tied to the balance of power between opposing sides. In the world wars of the 20th century, the materially inferior side embraced short-war thinking and staked its strategy on the rapid, destructive blow.[8] Because the opposing side possessed overall superior resources, the world wars devolved into struggles of attrition and the weaker side was decisively defeated.[9] Catastrophic great power wars prior to the 20th century were the result of the strategic miscalculation that a war against a materially superior power or coalition of powers can be won quickly and decisively. In more-recent military conflicts, such as in Iraq, Libya, the former Yugoslavia, Georgia, and Ukraine (2014), the destructive actions of the stronger side indeed led to decisive battle, even if the subsequent peace proved elusive in nearly every case.

The Nuclear Question

The impact of nuclear weapons on the destruction-attrition framework has been consequential. There is ambiguity in the character of future war between nuclear-armed great powers. Could such a war remain conventional and become protracted? Is it possible to have a strategy of destruction with the risks of nuclear escalation so high? If modern great power wars cannot be protracted, then might it be more prudent to have a conventional military force that could rapidly seize the initiative and strike the decisive, lightning blow to end the war quickly? History suggests that an adversary with ample means to fight back would likely have enough capacity to retaliate, rendering the initial logic faulty.

Soviet views on the character of future war and strategy in the nuclear era evolved over time. Eventually, the Soviets found that strategic nuclear parity increased the likelihood of a conventional phase of the war. Some circles believed that the war might remain conventional for some time, devolv-

---

[8] Nolan, 2017, pp. 572–578.

[9] Jean de Bloch wrote in the late 19th century about the relationship between the large economic potential of states and long wars of attrition. Bloch's analysis generally was correct, while his conclusion about the impossibility of such a catastrophic war unfortunately was not. See Jean de Bloch, *The Future of War in Its Technical, Economic, and Political Relations*, trans. R. C. Long, Boston, Mass.: Ginn and Company, 1903.

ing into a protracted conflict.[10] Until the mid-1980s, Soviet strategy nevertheless focused on destruction through the strategic offensive with reserves at the ready to build on the acquired offensive momentum. General-Major Vasilii Burenok and Yurii Pechatnov, leading Russian military theorists, summarized the predominant Soviet views on the character of future war during the Cold War period:

> For most of the [post–World War II] period, Soviet military doctrine assumed that a war between the United States and the USSR [Union of Soviet Socialist Republics or Soviet Union] would lead to the use of nuclear weapons. In fact, until the 1960s in the publications of the official circles of the USSR, there was a conviction that the only possible conflict between the USSR and the United States would be a large-scale nuclear war. In the late 60s and early 70s, the military-strategic parity achieved between the USSR and the United States, the Warsaw Pact and NATO, led to revision of doctrinal guidelines. Thereafter, official Soviet doctrine began to allow for the possibility of a phased war in Europe, in which the first phase could be fought with conventional forces.
>
> Throughout the 1970s and 1980s, Soviet experts and representatives of the military circles disputed the inevitability of nuclear escalation, allowing for the possibility of a large, protracted war between East and West in which nuclear weapons would not be used. In the 1980s, the Military Doctrine of the USSR began to highlight the potential for nuclear deterrence, considering [nuclear weapons] as a means of retaliation.[11]

The Conventional Theater Operation

The debate over conventional great power war intensified throughout the 1970s. Technological advances were poised to bring about consequential

---

[10] David M. Glantz, *The Military Strategy of the Soviet Union: A History*, Frank Cass and Co., 1992, p. 199.

[11] V. M. Burenok and Iu. A. Pechatnov, *Strategicheskoe sderzhivanie*, prepublication copy, 2011, pp. 20–21.

changes to military affairs. The nascent information technology revolution at that time was so promising that the Soviets likely "adopted an independent conventional war option as a long-term development goal."[12] This goal was most prominently promoted by the then–Chief of the General Staff, Nikolai Ogarkov. After conducting several years of exercises that experimented with new operational concepts, Ogarkov updated the operational planning manuals with particular attention devoted to strategic operations in the military theater and missile defense.[13] Ogarkov asserted that Western technological developments would allow the United States to prioritize conventional weapons over nuclear ones, which might undermine deterrence or create escalation dilemmas for the Soviets in a future war.[14] In the years that followed, the Soviets continued to investigate the problem of dealing with an adversary that could inflict increasing levels of damage in the initial period of war with conventional precision munitions.[15] In fact, the threat of NATO long-range conventional attack remains the central military problem facing Russian planners to this day.

At the same time when Ogarkov was espousing his views on the "stability" of conventional war versus the unpredictability and futility of nuclear war, there was growing appreciation in the Soviet analytical community of the consequences of nuclear war. Advanced models had been developed within the Main Intelligence Directorate in the early 1970s to consider the possibility of nuclear escalation control and the second- and third-order effects of nuclear strikes.[16] The destructive power of nuclear weapons made them useful for deterrence tasks but were perhaps of limited utility otherwise. Mary FitzGerald and Raymond Garthoff, close observers of Soviet military policy, respectively concluded that by the mid-1980s the Soviets had determined that even limited nuclear war could be resistant to escala-

---

[12] Mary FitzGerald, "Marshal Ogarkov and the Modern Theater Operation," *Naval War College Review*, Vol. 39, No. 4, Autumn 1986b, p. 7.

[13] M. A. Moiseev, "Strategicheskie zadeli Marshala Ogarkova," *Krasnaia zvezda*, October 26, 2007.

[14] FitzGerald, 1986b, pp. 39–58.

[15] Glantz, 1992, p. 201.

[16] Vitalii Tsygichko, *Models in the System of Strategic Decisions in the USSR*, Lambert Academic Publishing, 2017, pp. 13–17.

tion control.[17] As a result, by the 2010s, the idea that Russia had to embrace trends in conventional precision strike to provide greater flexibility in strategic deterrence in the 21st century became relatively mainstream.

Destruction and Attrition in Modern Conditions

The confluence of greater appreciation of the unacceptable consequences of nuclear use with the NATO development of more precise conventional options has raised questions on the destruction-attrition approach to strategy.[18] Decisive destruction between nuclear powers could theoretically occur through a decapitating first strike using nuclear weapons to render any meaningful retaliation impossible. Russian statements and doctrine have been consistent that Russia does not plan to preemptively destroy an adversary with strategic nuclear weapons.[19] Nor is there any evidence that Russia believes it can win such a war at an acceptable cost.[20]

An attrition strategy at the strategic nuclear level is not viable for Russia (or any nuclear power). Given the number of nuclear weapons in the inventories of NATO countries, there is no question of exhausting the West of its munitions while inflicting sufficient damage on critical targets and advancing personnel. If each side accepts that strategic nuclear weapons use could only lead to mutual assured destruction and an inability to achieve the political aims of the war, then a conventional option to destroy (or disable) an assigned number of critical military and civilian targets in the initial period of war is preferable. Conventional defensive operations in the initial period of war are conceivable for Russia.[21] This strategy might involve

---

[17] Mary FitzGerald, *Changing Soviet Doctrine on Nuclear War*, Alexandria, Va.: Center for Naval Analyses, October 1986a, pp. 26–29; Garthoff is cited within the FitzGerald piece.

[18] Marina Eliseeva, "Uroki na vse vremena," *Krasnaia zvezda*, October 27, 2010.

[19] Valdai Discussion Club, "Vladimir Putin Meets with Members of the Valdai Discussion Club," event transcript, webpage, October 18, 2018.

[20] Mikhail Rostovskii, "Sergei Shoigu rasskazal, kak spasali rossiiskuiu armiiu," *Moskovskii komsomolets*, September 22, 2019.

[21] Kokoshin and Larionov (1991, p. 8) summarized Svechin's views on the definition of attrition: "Defense, disquieting actions, achievement of success by means of winning a number of small successes in order to combine them in the long run into a general over-

the development of sufficient capabilities to attrit and exhaust the forces and means involved in the expected aerospace attack against Russia while accepting greater losses of critical military and nonmilitary infrastructure within Russia or in allied countries. In theory, Russia would hope to retain sufficient capacity to build up military strength to launch a counteroffensive in Europe to achieve assigned war aims. The critical assessment in this case is *whether the attacking side possesses the means to achieve a decisive outcome.*

Table 1.1 presents the situational factors that often are influential on a country's military strategy. We selected these factors based on a review of literature on military strategy (see Sources section of this chapter). A favorable balance of power typically favors a destructive strategy, whereas an economically and technologically stronger opponent theoretically suggests an approach of battle avoidance or exhausting the stronger attacking side so that the second phase of the war is fought with more-favorable force correlations. Diplomacy is also a way to mitigate weakness as well as a dual flank threat in the case of countries without protective natural boundaries (e.g., Russia).

TABLE 1.1

Situational Factors That Influence Destruction and Attrition Strategies

Situational Factor	Destruction	Attrition
Balance of power	Militarily weaker opponent	Economically, technologically stronger opponent; diplomacy to mitigate power imbalance and dual flank threat
Future war	Forecast of quick war (days to six months)	Expectation of protracted war (more than six months)

SOURCE: Adapted from Aleksandr A. Svechin, *Strategy*, Kent D. Lee, ed., Minneapolis, Minn.: East View Publications, 1991; and Nolan, 2017.
NOTE: Strategies can change after the war begins based on the circumstances. We are interested in the starting point, how a country is devising strategy and organizing operations for future war. The indicators in this table form our approach to determine the orientation of military strategy.

all victory." See also Jacob Kipp, "General-Major A. A. Svechin and Modern Warfare: Military History and Military Theory," in Aleksandr A. Svechin, *Strategy*, Kent D. Lee, ed., Minneapolis, Minn.: East View Publications, 1992, pp. 23–60.

An overwhelming power balance usually leads to a forecast of a quick war terminated in weeks or a few months. An unfavorable balance of power in most cases rules out a quick war initiated by the weaker side, although the fallacy has been a tempting and consequential one. Adolf Hitler believed that the Soviet Union could be decisively defeated in a matter of weeks. Japan in 1941 was a more nuanced case in which at least some military and political leaders did not think victory was possible over any duration but launched the war anyway out of desperation.[22] Indeed, as we explain in the following paragraphs, the factors and actions in Table 1.1 guide and begin our analysis of Russian military strategy, which might not fit neatly into a particular column.

A forecast of a rapid or protracted war against a specific opponent generally should have certain implications for force structure and operational planning. If war is not expected to last long, then a large and ready mobilization system probably will not be a priority. Rather, permanently ready forces who can move quickly to overwhelm the weaker side are the most sensible. Operations will be destructive and offensive to deprive the inferior opponent of any chance of victory.

Report Organization and Scope

Tables 1.1 and 1.2 show the structure of the report, which explores ways in which Russia is attempting to mitigate perceived weakness through military strategy.[23] The definition of *military strategy* that we use in this report is "the art of combining preparations for war and the [organization] of operations for achieving the goal set by the war for the armed forces."[24]

This report is organized into three chapters that follow this introductory chapter. Chapter Two identifies the prevailing Russian views on the first two situational factors. We also examine Russian diplomacy toward China, which we view as an important part of Russian strategy to both improve the power balance and preclude a dual flank threat. We are most interested in

---

[22] Lawrence Freedman, *The Future of War: A History*, New York: PublicAffairs, 2017, pp. 63–65.

[23] The factors and actions are guides for our analysis, not conclusions.

[24] Svechin, 1991, p. 69.

TABLE 1.2

Strategy Actions in Response to Situational Factors

Strategy Action	Destruction	Attrition
Force structure trends	Quantitative-qualitative superiority in ready ground, air, and naval forces to overwhelm adversary; ready state of nuclear and nonnuclear deterrence forces	Sufficient forces for defensive operations in initial period of war; ready state of nuclear forces
Mobilization activities	Greater emphasis on readiness across peacetime armed forces; less on large-scale state mobilization	Gradual but extensive mobilization plan to augment smaller, less-ready force
Organization of operations	Operational plan to destroy main enemy forces in initial period of war	Operational plan to conduct initial defense and counterattack

Russian ideas about how the balance of power (taking China into account) is impacting its views on future war. Even if the balance of power is not in its favor, does Russia believe that its large material resources and population of 144 million can either prevail or be defeated in a matter of weeks or months? Does Russia believe in decisive battle among great powers? The question of decisiveness in modern warfare is a crucial driver for other actions that Russia will take in force structure, mobilization, and operational planning.

Chapter Three explores force structure and mobilization trends. We investigate whether there is consistency in Russian rhetoric on the character of future war and force structure and mobilization actions. The expectation of a protracted war would lead to a greater emphasis on mobilization readiness and perhaps less on permanent readiness. If the war is going to be brief and happen without much warning, readiness will be paramount.

Chapter Four considers Russia's existing operational concepts in the context of the situational factors and actions that Russia is taking in force and mobilization readiness. Our assumption is that Russia will forecast the character of future war while considering the balance of power, build a force that corresponds to the forecast, and develop operational concepts to use those forces in expected future war scenarios. For example, Russia could view itself as the weaker power, while at the same time believing that it possesses enough resources that the attacking side will not be decisive in the initial period. This connotes a longer war that would allow for the possibility of strategic defensive operations in the initial period of war. The intent of this defensive approach would be to exhaust the stronger side of its advantages and transition to the next phase of the war with more-favorable force ratios (particularly in the aerospace domain).

Our analysis might not arrive at an unambiguous determination of Russian military strategy that falls neatly within the destruction-attrition dichotomy. Russia likely will not rigidly adhere to one side or the other in its military strategy. Destruction or attrition is more likely to be a guiding principle with some internal inconsistencies. There were some contradictions in Soviet military strategy that made it difficult for outside observers to correctly make sense of "a defensive policy with an offensive strategy."[25] But the analysis could inform plans to counter some components of Russian military strategy while perhaps giving less priority to others.

Scope

In this report, we are exclusively interested in the ways in which Russia, from a position of overall weakness, is planning and organizing conventional operational concepts for the initial period of war. Because we are limiting our analysis to the factors and actions in Tables 1.1 and 1.2, many important questions are left for other research to explore. For example, we do not cover the role of the military-industrial complex in driving procurement. Internal security and the role of the National Guard at home and abroad are generally beyond the scope of this work.[26] Information confrontation, Russia's fear of color revolutions at home, and other such topics that are relevant in Russian planning are not found in this report.[27] As mentioned previously,

---

[25] Interview with Soviet military expert, April 2021.

[26] There are some indications that some National Guard troops could have a role in an occupation of territory outside Russia, although we avoid discussion of that issue in this report. We conducted a separate study on Russia's ability to seize and hold territory in which we examined the tasks of the National Guard in a scenario (Anthony Atler and Scott Boston, unpublished RAND Corporation research, 2020).

[27] For a study on Russian views of information confrontation, see Michelle Grisé, Alyssa A. Demus, Yuliya Shokh, Marta Kepe, Jonathan Welburn, and Khrystyna Holynska, *Rivalry in the Information Sphere: Russian Conceptions of Information Confrontation*, Santa Monica, Calif.: RAND Corporation, RR-A198-8, 2022.

the role of nuclear weapons in Russian military strategy is undoubtedly important. Russian conventional operations are undergirded by the threat of nuclear use, but this applies to NATO as well.[28] Addressing the question of how much each side would be influenced by the other's nuclear capability is a complicated task that we do not undertake in this work.

Sources

This report is influenced most of all by two works. The first is *Strategy*, published in 1927 (an English translation was published in 1991) by the Soviet strategist Aleksandr Svechin. The book is relevant because our focus is on the organization of operations for the initial period of war in the context of overall power disparity, which was the critical issue for Svechin in the 1920s. It is not our starting assumption that the Russian military today adheres to the principles of Svechin. Rather *Strategy* presents a framework by which to analyze military strategy in the context of a power imbalance.

There are additional reasons to apply Svechin to the research question. Svechin remains relevant in contemporary Russian military thought at the highest levels of the military. The Chief of the General Staff, General Valerii Gerasimov, has referenced Svechin in four of his seven speeches before the Academy of Military Sciences since 2013. In a 2019 speech, Gerasimov invoked Svechin in the context of a discussion on the intersection of military strategy and economics. Other leading Russian military thinkers have similarly argued that Svechin's views remain relevant to Russian military strategy in the 21st century.[29] Finally, as we mention later in this report, the Chief of the Main Operations Directorate weighed in on the issue of destroying versus exhausting the opponent in a 2015 speech, and senior

---

[28] A curiosity of current discourse on Russia and NATO is that, in notional scenarios, Russian nuclear weapons are often assumed to be highly problematic for NATO and a significant deterrent, while NATO's nuclear capability has less influence on Russian decisionmakers.

[29] Kokoshin and Larionov, 1991, pp. 1–15; A. A. Kokoshin, *Vydaiushchiiisia voennyi teoretik i voenachal'nik Aleksandr Andreevich Svechin. O ego zhizni, ideiakh, trudakh i nasledii dlia nastoiashchego i budushchego*, Moscow: Izdatel'stvo Moskovskogo universiteta, 2013; and Kh. I. Saifetdinov, "Aleksandr Andreevich Svechin – vydaiushchiiisia voennyi myslitel' nachala XX veka," *Voennaia mysl'*, No. 8, 2018.

researchers from the 46th Central Scientific Research Institute of the Ministry of Defense (MoD) in a 2018 book alluded to a debate on the question within Russian military circles. All of this suggested to us that Svechin's views and thinking about strategy remained relevant, even if senior Russian military officers do not necessarily embrace his ideas.

The second work is *The Allure of Battle*, published in 2017 by the military historian Cathal Nolan. Read together with *Strategy*, there is a fair amount of consistency among the overarching ideas. Nolan's thesis is that short war thinking and an obsession with offensive battlefield tactics led to a catastrophic disregard for high-level military strategy. In the historical cases of the weaker side, Nolan contends that strategy was best pursued by battle avoidance, defense, and a willingness to embrace attrition if required. Both Svechin and Nolan agree, along with de Bloch, that material resources have been a crucial factor in strategy and warfare of the past two centuries. An underestimation of the material and spiritual resiliency of the adversary, combined with short-war delusions, is what Nolan urges to avoid and deter in modern state competition.

The remainder of our sources were largely drawn from Russian military literature. We consulted defense periodicals, official military and military science journals, and authoritative books on military strategy. Our approach, which relied only on open sources, began by consulting the views of the most senior Russian military officers: Chiefs of the General Staff, Chiefs of the Main Operations Directorate, current officers within the Main Operations Directorate, retired General Staff officers, and senior researchers at such Russian military science institutions as the 46th Central Scientific Research Institute and the Russian Academy of Missile and Artillery Sciences. We then explored the Russian military literature to broaden our understanding of ideas raised by the aforementioned individuals. Because this report uses publicly available information, there are limitations to what we can learn about Russian operational concepts.

CHAPTER TWO

Situational Factors That Influence Russian Military Strategy

Introduction

Situational factors influence military strategy. If Russia believes that the balance of power is not in its favor and that future war will be protracted, then we would expect Russia to place less emphasis on permanent readiness across its armed forces and more on an efficient mobilization system to fill out a smaller number of existing formations and build up reserve formations over time. A prediction of a brief, destructive war would require ready, superior forces to inflict a lightning blow. This chapter examines the situational factors that were described Chapter One, including Russian diplomacy in China, which is one way to mitigate the perceived power imbalance.

Balance of Power

The geopolitical landscape in Europe has changed dramatically at the expense of Russia since 1991. The territory and population under the Kremlin's influence were greatly reduced as its alliance structure crumbled. Today, according to several Russian academic and MoD studies, Russia significantly trails the largest NATO countries (the United States, Germany, France, and the United Kingdom) across every indicator of state power, apart from *spiritual potential* (the will to fight).[1]

---

[1] Reach et al., 2022.

State power and military potential are the primary indicators that determine the balance of power among states. In the leadup to war, each side will need to consider how to organize operations based on what the enemy can bring to bear over given time periods. Table 2.1 depicts the full comparison using indicators of state power and assessments of advantage from Russian literature. Figure 2.1 summarizes the results of various Russian assessments and forecasts of military potential completed from 2012 to 2018.[2]

The Russian study and consideration of state power and military potential in long-term planning and threat assessments has implications for strategy. In peacetime, each side of the competition must constantly monitor the buildup of military capability of the other side and respond accordingly in force structure decisions. Russian military strategy is directed toward the management of the relative power and military potential of the opposing side.

Russian Diplomacy with China

One of the most common ways for a country to mitigate weakness against a stronger competitor has been to form an alliance with other powers to create a semblance of balance. However, Russia, as a great power, values "independence" above all in its foreign policy.[3] The Kremlin does not want to consult or rely on other powers prior to making decisions in defense of national interests. It desires freedom of maneuver. Russia's relationship with China has therefore been an intriguing one, particularly considering the balance of power and fallout with the West in 2014. Relative Russian weakness creates a possible contradiction between Russia's desire for independence on the one hand and for balance in the international system on the other. This section examines the nature of Russia's diplomacy with China to assess the sus-

---

[2] Reach et al., 2022.

[3] By *independence*, we mean that Russia will conduct foreign policy as it sees fit without having to consult with or rely on another power. The opposites of independence, in the Russian view, are NATO vassals, which do not have the military clout or confidence to make independent foreign policy decisions.

TABLE 2.1

Indicators and Comparison of State Power: North Atlantic Treaty Organization and Russia

Indicator	Characteristics	Russian Assessment of Advantage
Leadership	Ability to manage; trust of society; effectiveness of elite education; ability to achieve assigned objectives	N/A
Territory	Total area of territory; length of land and maritime borders of the state	NATO
Natural resources	Condition and amount of mineral, land, and water resources; existence of hospitable climate to support human activity	NATO
Population	Population size; health and demographic trends of the population	NATO
Economy	Total and per capita GDP and GNP; share of global economy; trade balance; purchasing power of national currency; character of imports and exports	NATO
Culture and religion	Contribution of the state to global culture; presence of religious centers of regional or global significance; degree of influence of national religious centers on global religion; degree of interfaith harmony in society	NATO[a]
Science and education	Level of development of critical technologies, including information; level of education standards; literacy among population; share of students pursuing higher education	NATO[a]
Armed forces	Existence and quality of strategic nuclear weapons and nuclear triad; level of development of general-purpose forces; sophistication and unification of command, control, and communications system; number of precision weapon systems	NATO
Foreign policy	Consistency; degree of aggressiveness; correspondence to national interests	N/A

SOURCE: Adapted from V. M. Burenok, ed., *Kontseptiia obosnovaniia perspektivnogo oblika silovykh komponentov voennoi organizatsii Rossiiskoi Federatsii*, Moscow: Granitsa Publishing House, 2018a, pp. 298–299.
NOTES: GDP = gross domestic product; GNP = gross national product; N/A = not applicable. Unless otherwise cited, assessments of advantage were made by authors using objective indicators, such as size of territory and GDP.
[a] Reach et al., 2022.

FIGURE 2.1

Summary of Military Potential Assessments and Forecasts from Russian Literature

Author(s)	Period of Assessment	Economic Potential	Military Potential	Political Potential	Moral/ Cultural/ Spiritual Potential	Overall Ranking in Power/ Position
Burenok, 2018b	2018	1. China 2. U.S. 3. Russia	Military-political potential 1. U.S. 2. China 3. Russia		1. Russia 2. U.S. 3. China	1. U.S. 2. China 3. Russia
	2025 (average across scenarios)	Not provided				1. U.S. 2. China 3. Russia
	2040 (average across scenarios)					1. China 2. U.S. 3. Russia
Buravlev, 2016	2016	1. U.S. 2. China 3. Russia	1. U.S. 2. Russia. 3. China	1. U.S. 2. China 3. Russia	Not provided	1. U.S. 2. China 3. Russia
Vinokurov, Kovalev, and Malkov, 2013, as summarized by Kovalev, 2014	2025	Not provided	1. NATO 2. China 3. Russia	Not provided	Not provided	1. NATO 2. China 3. Russia
Ageev, Mensch, and Matthews, eds., 2012	2012	1. U.S. 2. China 3. Russia	1. U.S. 2. Russia. 3. China	1. China 2. U.S. 3. Russia	1. U.S. and China 2. Russia	1. U.S. 2. China 3. Russia
	2030	1. U.S. 2. China 3. Russia	1. Russia 2. U.S. 3. China	1. U.S. 2. China 3. Russia	1. U.S. and China 2. Russia	1. U.S. 2. China 3. Russia

SOURCES: From Reach et al., 2022; compiled using the rankings presented in the analysis of Burenok, 2018b; A. I. Buravlev, "K voprosu ob otsenke moguchchestva gosudarstva," *Vooruzhenie i ekonomika*, No. 1, 2016; V. I. Kovalev, "Iadernoe bezopasnosti Rossii v XXI veke," Strategicheskaia stabil'nost', Vol. 3, No. 68, 2014, pp. 16–17; and A. I. Ageev, G. Mensch, and R. Matthews, eds., *Global Rating of Integral Power of 100 Countries 2012*, 3rd ed., Moscow: International Futures Research Academy, Institute for Economic Strategies, 2012.

NOTE: Selected indicators of military potential include literacy rate, GDP, territory, population, manpower of armed forces, mobilization potential, combat potential of service branches, and defense budget.

tainability of the relationship, which could have an influence on the future development of Russian military strategy.[4]

With similar ambitions of being a global power, China possesses the largest standing military in the world. The Chinese armed forces are composed of roughly 2 million personnel, dwarfing those of Russia.[5] China consistently devotes 1.9 percent of its GDP to military spending, which in 2019 equated to $266.4 billion. Russia, by contrast, spent $64.1 billion. Every year over the past decade, China has spent three to four times more on its armed forces relative to Russia.[6] Although some of this disparity should be expected because standing Chinese forces are twice as large as those of Russia, these sustained spending levels demonstrate that China is in earnest about its ambition to become a "world class power" by 2049.[7] China's comparatively limitless reserves of manpower combined with large reserves in materiel and arms suggest a large-scale conventional conflict between the two would be devastating for Russia.[8]

Conventional wisdom suggests these factors create the conditions for Moscow and Beijing to have a highly competitive, if not overtly hostile, relationship.[9] Yet, in June 2019, Russia and China jointly described their

---

[4] Japan is another key player in the region and its dispute with Russia over ownership of the Kuril Islands theoretically could become a flashpoint for conflict. Russian forecasts do not rule out this possibility. At the same time, China is the most important power in the region, and the military resources Russia would have to devote to parry a Chinese attack would be the most impactful on Russian military strategy. Understanding that Russia will need to manage its dispute with Japan, we focus our attention on China as the most consequential relationship for Russia given its relative weakness.

[5] Office of the Secretary of Defense, *Military and Security Developments Involving the People's Republic of China 2020: Annual Report to Congress*, Washington, D.C.: U.S. Department of Defense, 2020, p. 38.

[6] China Power, "What Does China Really Spend on Its Military?" webpage, Center for Strategic and International Studies, updated September 15, 2020.

[7] State Council Information Office of the People's Republic of China, *China's National Defense in the New Era*, July 24, 2019.

[8] Mary C. FitzGerald, "China's Evolving Military Juggernaut," in *China's New Great Leap Forward: High Technology and Military Power in the Next Half-Century*, Washington, D.C.: Hudson Institute, 2005, pp. 82–83.

[9] U.S.-China Economic and Security Review Commission, "Section 2: An Uneasy Entente: China-Russia Relations in a New Era of Strategic Competition with the United

relationship as a "comprehensive strategic partnership of coordination in a new era."[10] The strength and longevity of this partnership undoubtedly affects Russia's strategic calculus. That strategic calculus has been to protect its southern flank and avoid being isolated by the West by banding with China. Continued cooperation is a political decision, however, and it is prudent to consider the future of this relationship and its implications for NATO. This section of the analysis therefore considers the Sino-Russian relationship, providing a brief background of the history between the two neighbors, examining the facets that unify them and the issues that most plausibly divide them. Leveraging that analysis, we will make some conjectures about the prospects for a full-fledged alliance between the two states, the sustainability of their partnership, and whether the partnership poses a problem for the United States and NATO in the short- to medium-term.

Background

The centuries-long bilateral relationship between Russia and China can best be described as one of asymmetry. That asymmetry usually favored Russia. Vast territories were conceded to Russia at China's expense in the late 19th century, which allowed for Russia's expansion to the Pacific coast.[11] Communist ideology reunited the two states in common cause in the 1940s, but competition for global leadership of the communist movement resulted in a short-lived détente.[12] After a brief but bloody border clash in 1969, the relationship between the two countries remained strained until the mid-1980s. The discord was largely driven by Beijing's fears of encirclement given the Soviet invasion of Afghanistan and the Soviet Union's ties with a perennial

---

States," in *Report to Congress: U.S. China Economic and Security Review Commission*, Washington, D.C.: U.S. Government Publishing Office, November 2019.

[10] Office of the Secretary of Defense, 2020, p. 125.

[11] Immanuel C. Y. Hsu, *The Rise of Modern China*, New York: Oxford University Press, 1970, pp. 265–269.

[12] Christina Yeung and Nebojsa Bjelakovic, "The Sino-Russian Strategic Partnership: Views from Beijing and Moscow," *Journal of Slavic Military Studies*, Vol. 23, No. 2, 2010, p. 245.

Chinese foe, Vietnam.[13] The rise of more-pragmatic leaders in both countries allowed for a full normalization of bilateral relations by 1991, and in
the subsequent decades, the rapprochement between Moscow and Beijing
has flourished.

Since that time, though, the previously mentioned balance of power
between Russia and China has shifted precipitously, culminating in an
asymmetry that now politically and economically favors China.[14] Russia's
annexation of Crimea and subsequent sanctions imposed on it by the West
further widened the power gap; China's GDP doubled to eight times that of
Russia between 2013 and 2017.[15] However, economic and security cooperation between Moscow and Beijing increased significantly over this period.
Although perhaps counterintuitive, given that China's economic expansion
poses an undeniable challenge to Russian primacy in the region, the absence
of an alternative source for political and economic support narrowed Russia's room for maneuver.[16] Recent events, including the U.S.-China trade
war, the coronavirus disease 2019 (COVID-19) pandemic, and the collapse
of oil prices further exacerbated the economic asymmetry within the partnership. Paradoxically, these developments also elevated the importance of
Russia within the relationship as China pursued Russia's diplomatic support
in its various economic and political disputes with the United States.[17]

Sources of Synergy

International relations theory suggests that two proximate, ambitious, heavily armed states are much more likely to experience conflict than cooper-

---

[13] Yeung and Bjelakovic, 2010, p. 246.

[14] Jeronim Perović and Benno Zogg, "Russia and China: The Potential of Their Partnership," CSS Analyses in Security Policy, Center for Security Studies, ETH Zurich,
No. 250, October 2019.

[15] Marcin Kaczmarski, Mark N. Katz, and Teija Tiilikainen, The Sino-Russian and
US-Russian Relationships: Current Developments and Future Trends, No. 57, Helsinki:
Finish Institute of International Affairs, December 2018, p. 23.

[16] Kaczmarski, Katsz, and Tiilikainen, 2018, p. 25.

[17] Yaroslav Trofimov and Thomas Grove, "Weary Russia Tries to Avoid Entanglement
in US-China Spat," Wall Street Journal, June 22, 2020.

ation.[18] Common interests along several political, economic, and military fronts have nonetheless combined to facilitate a partnership. Moscow and Beijing share a primary focus: political regime security. Neither state views the other as a threat to regime survival; rather they share the view that the source of the threat arises from the West and its supposed fomenting of color revolutions with the objective of regime change.[19] Russia's annexation of Crimea and China's adventurism in the South China Sea, to name just a few sources of friction with the West, has resulted in Russia and China finding themselves with few alternative potential allies who possess significant international power or stature.[20] Moreover, both states reject the continuation of an international order dominated by the United States and its allies, favor noninterference, and reject the primacy of liberal democratic value systems of governance.[21] These well-aligned domestic and geopolitical interests form the backbone of the Russian-Chinese partnership.

With respect to the economic sphere, Russia and China find themselves similarly aligned, if unequally dependent on one another. China possesses a voracious appetite for natural resources, in particular oil and gas. Russia possesses a large, proximate supply of both commodities. In 2016, Russia surpassed Saudi Arabia as China's largest single supplier of crude oil, and following the completion of the *Power of Siberia* pipeline, Russia obtained the capacity to also become China's largest supplier of liquified natural gas.[22] Trade with China thus provided Russia an essential economic lifeline in the wake of the economic sanctions imposed on Russia following its invasion of Ukraine.[23] For its part, prior to escalating tariffs imposed on imports of U.S. liquefied natural gas, the United States was China's third-largest sup-

---

[18] See, for example, Kenneth N. Waltz, *Theory of International Politics*, Reading, Mass: Addison-Wesley Publishing Company, 1979; and John J. Mearsheimer, *The Tragedy of Great Power Politics*, New York: W. W. Norton and Company, 2001.

[19] Kaczmarski, Katz, and Tiilikainen, 2018, p. 26.

[20] Samuel Charap, John Drennan, and Pierre Noël, "Russia and China: A New Model of Great-Power Relations," *Survival*, Vol. 59, No. 1, February–March 2017, pp. 26–27.

[21] Perović and Zogg, 2019, p. 1.

[22] Erica Downs, "China-Russia Energy Relations: Why the Power of Siberia Pipeline Matters to China," blog post, CNA, December 19, 2019.

[23] Charap, Drennan, and Noël, 2017, p. 28.

plier. Russian pipelines thus plausibly provide a more reliable and proximate supply of crucial resources to China.[24]

Finally, in the military domain, China and Russia have found additional incentives for cooperation. Having been cut off from accessing Western arms in the wake of the 1989 Tiananmen Square massacre, the modernization of China's military has flowed largely through Moscow.[25] Since the collapse of the Soviet Union, Russia has sold China an array of advanced armaments, including combat aircraft, helicopters, submarines, destroyers, surface-to-air missile (SAM) batteries, and radar.[26] Chinese attempts to reverse-engineer Russian technology and recruit Russian scientists eventually dampened Russia's willingness to continue transferring arms to China, and exports of complex weapons systems were halted for more than a decade.[27] However, it is possible that in the wake of China's failure to replicate the U.S. F-22, even after extensive industrial and cyber espionage, Russia decided the risks of cooperation were tolerable.[28] In 2016, Russia completed delivery of 24 Su-35s, Russia's most-advanced fourth-generation fighter aircraft, and agreed to sell China eight S-400 long-range SAM systems.[29]

Of course, military cooperation within the partnership is not limited to arms sales. Since 2005, Russia and China have engaged in many joint exercises, including land, naval, anti-missile, and internal security exercises.[30] A qualitative upgrade in Russian-Chinese military cooperation occurred in 2018, when roughly 3,000 Chinese troops, 900 tanks and military vehicles,

---

[24] Downs, 2019.

[25] Yeung and Bjelakovic, 2010, p. 257.

[26] Stockholm International Peace Research Institute, "SIPRI Arms Transfers Database," webpage, last updated March 15, 2021.

[27] Yeung and Bjelakovic, 2010, p. 258; and Kaczmarski, Katz, and Tiilikainen, 2018, p. 36.

[28] Andrea Gilli and Mauro Gilli, "Why China Has Not Caught Up Yet: Military-Technological Superiority and the Limits of Imitation, Reverse Engineering, and Cyber Espionage," *International Security*, Vol. 43, No. 3, Winter 2018/19, pp. 180–183.

[29] Office of the Secretary of Defense, 2020, p. 51.

[30] Kaczmarski, Katz, and Tiilikainen, 2018, pp. 37–38.

and 30 fixed-wing aircraft and helicopters participated in Vostok 2018.[31] China's involvement represented the first time that a non-Collective Security Treaty Organization (CSTO) state participated in one of Russia's four strategic command-staff capstone exercises.[32] Subsequently, China has taken part in Tsentr 2019, several joint aviation patrols (including long-range bomber patrols) and live-fire air defense exercises at sea.[33] These activities certainly demonstrate multidimensional military cooperation. However, Russian and Chinese forces have yet to demonstrate an interoperability between their forces that would make these exercises truly joint.[34]

Incentives for Independence

The interests of Moscow and Beijing very clearly align along numerous axes. Russia and China have intentional pursued ways to accommodate the interests of one another and have often succeeded, if at times by accident. However, sources of potential friction also abound. Growing Chinese influence in Central Asia, relative demographic trends, the history of Russia's Far East, and varying geostrategic objectives create significant incentives for *independence*—the ability to conduct foreign policy based on national interests without consulting the other side. The question is certainly open, though, as to whether Russia possesses plausible alternatives to increased accommodation and cooperation with China.

Russia, as always, remains focused on the balance of power within its perceived sphere of influence: Central Asia. China's influence in the region expanded considerably over the past two decades, and this influence has

---

[31] Dave Johnson, "VOSTOK 2018: Ten Years of Russian Strategic Exercises and Warfare Preparation," webpage, *NATO Review*, December 20, 2018.

[32] Angela Stent, "Russia and China: Axis of Revisionists?" Washington, D.C.: Brookings Institution, February 2020. The CSTO is an alliance that includes Armenia, Kazakhstan, Kyrgyzstan, Russia, and Tajikistan.

[33] Stent, 2020, p. 5; and, Franz-Stefan Gady, "China, Russia Conduct First Joint Live-Fire Missile Exercise at Sea," blog post, *The Diplomat*, May 8, 2019.

[34] U.S.-China Economic and Security Review Commission, 2019, p. 343.

come at Russia's expense.[35] Beijing now holds the economic pride of place in the region, usurping Russia as the region's largest lender, trading partner, and investor.[36] For its part, though, Beijing has gone out of its way to demonstrate self-restraint and to treat Russia as an equal power.[37] The two sides settled on a "division of labor" that cedes the security realm and influence over political issues to Russia while China dominates the economic space.[38] However, the sustainability of such an arrangement seems suspect. Assuming that Russia's economic prospects continue to deteriorate as the result of endemic corruption, China might find it untenable to rely on such a partner to protect its investments.[39] In 2017, for example, China constructed a military base in Tajikistan, purportedly for logistics and training purposes.[40] Should China decide that its interests require further encroachment within Russia's security realm, such a move would almost certainly strain— although perhaps not break—the strength of the Russo-Chinese partnership. Ultimately, whether the two powers eventually collide in Central Asia most likely depends on whether China continues to accommodate Russia's quest for great power status and "create the illusion of equality."[41]

Perennial Russian concerns about the vulnerability of its far east provide a second motivation for Russia to seek greater independence from China. Russian attempts to offer a counterweight to China in East Asia have largely

---

[35] Kaczmarski, Katz, and Tiilikainen, 2018, pp. 40–41.

[36] Kaczmarski, Katz, and Tiilikainen, 2018, p. 40.

[37] Dimitri Trenin, *True Partners? How Russia and China See Each Other*, Moscow: Centre for European Reform, Carnegie Moscow Center, 2012, pp. 16, 31.

[38] Andrew Radin, Lynn E. Davis, Edward Geist, Eugeniu Han, Dara Massicot, Matthew Povlock, Clint Reach, Scott Boston, Samuel Charap, William Mackenzie, Katya Migacheva, Trevor Johnston, and Austin Long, *The Future of the Russian Military: Russia's Ground Combat Capabilities and Implications for U.S.-Russia Competition*, Santa Monica, Calif.: RAND Corporation, RR-3099-A, 2019, p. 10.

[39] Perović and Zogg, 2019, p. 3.

[40] Stephen Blank, "China's Military Base in Tajikistan: What Does it Mean?" blog post, Central Asia-Caucus Analyst, April 18, 2019. China consulted closely with Russia on the construction of the base in Tajikistan, even asking whether it might be more palatable for Russia if the base were staffed by mercenaries rather than uniformed soldiers.

[41] Kaczmarski, Katz, and Tiilikainen, 2018, p. 59.

been failures, however. Russia lacks the political will to settle its territorial dispute over the Kuril Islands with Japan, lacks the leverage to ingratiate itself with North Korea (and thus has limited utility for South Korea), and is a significantly more-junior economic partner relative to China. Perhaps paradoxically, Moscow's attempt to challenge Beijing's primacy in the region created no change in their relationship, largely because of Russia's failure to compete.[42]

Two fears in particular motivated Russia's "turn to the east" in 2012. First, immigrant flows from Northeast China into the region feed the fear that a Chinese minority could eventually outnumber the Russian population, leading to succession and reunification with China.[43] Second, mirroring Russia's own claims of the right to intervene on behalf of ethnic Russians abroad, Russia fears that China might use a similar justification for military intervention in the region.[44] A 2003 book by Professor Yuri M. Galenovich, a Russian Sinologist, cited Chinese educational texts and maps that outline the Chinese territories that have been annexed by Russia as evidence of Chinese ambitions to reclaim this territory and expand its borders.[45] General-Major V. G. Slipchenko, the former head of the Scientific Research Department of the General Staff Academy, further raised the alarm about threatening Chinese objectives long-term, warning of a Chinese "Monroe Doctrine" in 2005.[46]

---

[42] Kaczmarski, Katz, and Tiilikainen, p. 48.

[43] Yeung and Bjelakovic, 2010, p. 270. The demographic disparity in the region has remained roughly the same over the past decade; there are 200 million inhabitants on the Chinese side of the border and only 8 million on the Russian side.

[44] Yeung and Bjelakovic, 2010, p. 270.

[45] Yuri M. Galenovich, *The Mandates of Jiang Zemin*, Moscow: Muravey, 2003, pp. 332–333. Galenovich is one of the leading figures at the Institute of the Far East in Moscow. He is a well-known Sinologist in Russia.

[46] FitzGerald, 2005, p. 85. For its part, current junior high school history textbooks in China recount Russia's "seizure" and "occupation" of vast amounts of Chinese land, taking advantage of the weakness of the Qing dynasty. These textbooks further emphasize the importance of not forgetting this time of national humiliation. See Dan Ting Li, Dararat Mattariganond, and Benjawan Narasaj, "The Opium Wars in China's Junior High School Textbooks," *Journal of Mekong Societies*, Vol. 15, No. 2, May–August 2019.

Finally, the long-term geopolitical aspirations of Russia and China diverge in meaningful ways. China seeks an open global economy (albeit open *to* China, if not the other way around). Russia, on the other hand, lacks a competitive edge and thus generally rejects globalization. Additionally, while China seeks to reshape the international order, Russia seeks to undermine it. China therefore engages more frequently in global governance and takes a much greater interest in the stability of the global economy. Russia finds great value in volatility. To the degree that Russia continues to foment instability in a quest to regain great power status (if only in the short-term), it is possible that cooperation between the two will be undermined. Of course, whatever path is taken will be fundamentally affected by how their individual relationships with the United States evolve in the coming decade.[47]

An Alliance or Axis of Convenience?

During the 1990s, debates over whether a newly emerging China represented a threat, partner, or something in between were overtaken by the first round of NATO enlargement. Prime Minister Yevgeniy Primakov's subsequent efforts to cultivate a relationship with China were met with widespread support.[48] Moreover, as already noted, economic and military cooperation between Russia and China has expanded dramatically post-2014. These events elicit three questions that this section will attempt to address, drawing on Russian academic and military literature. First, what are the future prospects for this partnership—i.e., given their shared interests, might Russia and China's relationship evolve into a true alliance? Second, is there a fundamental disconnect between the Russian military and political leadership with respect to the threat posed by China? Even if it remains a strategic partnership of convenience, how might this relationship affect the United States and NATO in a crisis or conflict scenario?

---

[47] Kaczmarski, Katz, and Tiilikainen, 2018, pp. 50–59.

[48] Sergei Troush, *Final Report: Russia's Responses to the NATO Expansion: China Factor,* NATO Democratic Institutions Fellowships 1997–1999 Final Report, Moscow, 1999. The mixed threat perception can be seen with the counter-programming of Russian Defense Minister Igor Rodionov's inclusion of China on the list of potential strategic adversaries. See "Defence Minister Rodionov Goes on the Warpath," *Izvestia,* December 27, 1996.

The general trend within the Kremlin has been a push for closer ties with China. In 2000, President Vladimir Putin declared China to be a "strategic partner" working with Russia in "all spheres of activity."[49] The Kremlin focused specifically on Moscow and Beijing's well-aligned geopolitical views: specifically, the preference for a multipolar, United Nations (UN)–centered global order (where both countries have veto power) and the existence of the dual threats of Islamic extremism and Western-backed regime change.[50] The 2001 creation of the Shanghai Cooperation Organization (SCO) reflected an effort to demonstrate tangible progress in the partnership.[51] However, Russia's leadership concurrently moved to shore up its security interests in Central Asia and balance against China, creating the CSTO in 2002 and reaching long-term bilateral agreements with Tajikistan and Kyrgyzstan on military basing rights.[52] More recently, Putin has consistently refuted assertions that China posed a threat to Russia and pressed instead for ever-closer ties, particularly in the wake of the 2014 sanctions on Russia by the West. The leadership of Russian parties throughout the political spectrum also publicly champions closer relations with Beijing.[53]

Russian military circles viewed China's rise with more skepticism. Concern within the military emphasized the disadvantageous shift in the conventional military balance and raised alarms about Chinese exercises that emphasized mobility and force projection.[54] In 2009, Lieutenant-General Sergey Skokov, the Chief of the Main Staff of the Russian Ground Forces, described an encircled Russia faced with "potential threats" from the west, east, and south.[55] While conspicuously leaving the enemy and scenario

---

[49] "Putin: China Is Strategic Partner," *UPI*, Moscow, July 16, 2000.

[50] Yeung and Bjelakovic, 2010, p. 271.

[51] Dmitri Trenin, "Kitai trebuet pristalnogo vnimania," Carnegie Center Moscow Briefing, Vol. 3, No. 5, May 2001.

[52] Yeung and Bjelakovic, 2010, p. 273.

[53] Anastasia Solomentseva, "The 'Rise' of China in the Eyes of Russia: A Source of Threat or New Opportunities?" *Connections*, Vol. 14, No. 1, Winter 2014.

[54] Solomentsova, 2014, pp. 17–19; Yeung and Bjelakovic, 2010, pp. 273-274.

[55] Roger N. McDermott, "Zapad 2009 Rehearses Countering a NATO Attack on Belarus," *Eurasia Daily Monitor*, Vol. 6, No. 179, September 30, 2009.

unspecified, Russia's first test of its military reforms in Vostok-2010 practiced the Russian armed forces' ability to halt and repel a mass conventional offensive into Siberia.[56] Since then, mentions of China as a security threat have been absent in open discussions by Russia's military.[57] Finally, rather than being its most plausible target, China participated in Vostok-2018.

In the academic and think-tank community, the vast majority of scholars advocate for a closer partnership between Moscow and Beijing. Within most circles, the idea of a "Chinese threat" is met with skepticism and caution.[58] Scholars from the Institute for Political and Military Analysis provide the main source of alarmist rhetoric that China poses a direct threat to Russia.[59] This radical wing regards a Chinese invasion to seize Siberia and the Far East—and thus secure its access to the resources for its growth—as a Chinese necessity and highly probable event.[60] One scholar from the Institute, A. Khramchikhin, opined about the haltingly slow transition to the T-14 Armata battle tank and the failure to acquire an "acceptable" number of tanks. Khramchikhin argues that the declarations that large-scale tank battles are relics of a bygone era do not reflect reality. He notes that tank battles against NATO are implausible because "NATO troops are not ready for such battles due to psychological reasons." However, he goes on the argue, tank battles will find their "most important" role in battles against Chinese People's Liberation Army (PLA) tanks.[61]

Rhetoric and military exercises aside, the prospects for a true alliance akin to NATO still seem scant. Neither government has openly supported the other's more-aggressive foreign policy moves. China has not recognized South Ossetia, Abkhazia, or Crimea. Moscow similarly remained neutral

---

[56] Roger N. McDermott, "Russian Military Prepares for Vostok 2010," *Eurasia Daily Monitor*, Vol. 7, No. 106, June 2, 2010.

[57] Dmitry (Dima) Adamsky, "If War Comes Tomorrow: Russian Thinking About 'Regional Nuclear Deterrence,'" *Journal of Slavic Military Studies*, Vol. 27, No. 1, 2014, p. 168.

[58] Solomentseva, 2014, p. 17.

[59] Solomentseva, 2014, p. 17.

[60] Solomentseva, 2014, pp. 17–18.

[61] Alexander Khramchikhin, "Prezhdevremennyi otkaz ot broni," *Nezavisamoye voennoye obozreniye*, February 20, 2020.

while China pursued territorial claims against Japan and built islands in the South China Sea.[62] Russia also conspicuously avoids selling certain types of military equipment to China. China has attempted, for example, to purchase aerial refueling tankers, strategic airlift assets, and submarines. Very few sales of such strategic offensive power projection systems have been approved.[63] The reportedly low level of intelligence-sharing between the two countries, and the absence of formal joint structures to enable interoperability similarly suggest a relationship that is not a formal alliance.[64] Finally, even in the wake of the qualitatively improved relationship between Moscow and Beijing in 2014, high-level military consultations and joint exercises have not reached the watermark that was set in 2005. If both states were keen to formalize their alliance, one would have expected the opposite to be the case.[65]

In terms of public statements addressing this question, in July 2014, the Chief of Russian presidential staff, Sergei Ivanov, stated that Russia and China would not "create a new military alliance, union or something like that."[66] More-recent statements by Putin characterized Sino-Russian ties as "an allied relationship in the full sense of a multifaceted strategic partnership."[67] China, though, rejects such language, referring instead to its "all-encompassing partnership and strategic interaction" with Russia.[68] For its part, official Chinese statements characterize military alliances as

---

[62] Kaczmarski, Katz, and Tiilikainen, 2018, p. 55.

[63] Yeung and Bjelakovic, 2010, p. 274; Stockholm International Peace Research Institute, 2021.

[64] Roger N. McDermott, "Russia's Impact on Nuclear Policy in China: Cooperative Trends and Depth of Influence," *Journal of Slavic Military Studies*, Vol. 33, No. 1, 2020a, pp. 50–51.

[65] McDermott, 2020a, pp. 64–65.

[66] "Russia, China Do Not Plan to Create Any Military Union - Russian Presidential Staff Chief," TASS, July 10, 2014.

[67] Vasily Kashin, "Russia and China Take Military Partnership to New Level," *Moscow Times*, October 23, 2019.

[68] Kashin, 2019.

Cold War relics that leave others insecure.[69] Formally declaring an alliance also entails numerous downsides and few (if any) benefits. At a minimum, a Sino-Russian alliance would "likely force their neighbors or regional rivals to seek to bolster their own military relationships with the Unites States."[70]

The COVID-19 pandemic also had a chilling effect on the partnership. Moscow quickly supported demands for an international inquiry into origins of the pandemic, irritating Chinese officials. Russia also swiftly closed its land border with China.[71] Additional affronts followed; first, there was a celebration of the 160th anniversary of the founding of the city of Vladivostok—the capital of the Chinese area annexed by Russia after the Second Opium Wars—which was followed by Russia finalizing an armaments deal with India in the midst of an Indo-Sino border clash.[72] Several prominent academics also publicly called further alignment with China a "strategic miscalculation" and urged the Kremlin to pursue a policy of "nonalignment" between China and the United States.[73]

These diplomatic and academic jabs played out in the wake of opportunistic moves by China. With the collapse of global oil demand as a result of the pandemic, Russia found the price of oil in freefall. China let its "partner" dangle, capitalizing on the opportunity to cheaply build its oil reserves by 1.15 billion barrels before curtailing its purchase of Middle Eastern oil in favor of Russian oil.[74] China thus maneuvered into a dominant position over Russia, cutting out other buyers while amassing strategic levels of reserves. This manipulation represents the exact behavior that observers argued could cause Moscow to reassess the partnership. Specifically, analysts have

---

[69] Xi Jinping, "New Asian Security Concept for New Progress in Security Cooperation," remarks at the Fourth Summit of the Conference on Interaction and Confidence Building Measures in Asia, Shanghai: Shanghai Expo Center, May 21, 2014.

[70] Yeung and Bjelakovic, 2010, p. 256.

[71] Trofimov and Grove, 2020.

[72] Stanislaw Skarzynski and Daniel Wong, "Is Putin's Russia Seeking a New Balance Between China and the West?" *The Diplomat*, August 28, 2020.

[73] Trofimov and Grove, 2020.

[74] Trofimov and Grove, 2020.

argued that such power plays could "generate resentment and a backlash in the Russian elite" at being relegated to the role of a "junior partner."[75]

This partnership is most certainly not a traditional defense alliance. Both sides prefer self-interest over loyalty and avoid engagement in those areas where their interests do not align.[76] Even if the United States continues to unite Russia and China against a shared enemy, it is difficult to see how this union is sustainable in the medium- to long-term. If China continues to capitalize on its dominant role, no longer pretending that this is a partnership between equals, it is not entirely implausible that Russia could look to extricate itself from the tiger's jaws. Russian fears of encirclement, loss of great power status, and a perception of a negative imbalance could thus even trigger a Russian pivot back toward the West.[77]

With respect to whether a disconnect exists between the Russian military and political elites regarding whether China poses a threat, some conjectures can be made that such is the case. A 2001 article in *Voyennaya mysl* argued that China represents "the main (and perhaps sole) threat to Russia."[78] In 2009, the Russian Army's chief of staff Lieutenant General Skokov described China as a "multi-million-strong force guided by traditional views to combat operations: straightforward, with massive concentration of manpower and firepower on key axes."[79] Because of the asymmetry in conventional forces, it is not implausible that Russia's military perceives a threat. In the years that have followed, though, mentions of China as a

---

[75] Kaczmarski, Katz, and Tillikainen, 2018, p. 59. See also Charap, Drennan, and Noël, 2017, p. 39.

[76] Jacob L. Shapiro, "Russia and China's Alliance of Convenience," blog post, *Geopolitical Futures*, December 26, 2017; and Richard J. Ellings and Robert Sutter, eds., *Axis of Authoritarians: Implications of China-Russia Cooperation*, Seattle, Wash.: National Bureau of Asian Research, 2018.

[77] Skarzynski and Wong, 2020. Such a pivot would parallel Russia's sharp turn toward China in 2002—fearing encirclement and regime change—in response to the U.S. invasion of Afghanistan and Iraq.

[78] A. F. Klimenko and V. I. Lutovinov, "We May Endanger Russia's Military Security by Misrepresenting Real Threats," *Voennaia mysl'*, No. 4, 2001.

[79] Trenin, 2012, p. 41.

source of threat to Russia disappeared from Russia's military writings and foreign policy doctrine.[80]

The purported "brain of the Russian Army," the Center for Military-Strategic Research under the General Staff (*Tsentr voyenno-strategicheskikh issledovaniy Generalnogo Shtaba Vooruzhennykh sil' Rossiyskoy federatsii—TsSVI GSh*) has consistently advocated for more robust defense ties between the two capitals.[81] In a 2004 chapter of a book issued by the TsSVI GSh titled *Voyennaya bezopasnost' rossiyskoy federatsii v xxi veke: sbornik nauchnykh statey* (*The Military Security of the Russian Federation in the Twenty-First Century*), the then–Chief of the General Staff Colonel-General Yury Baluyevskiy editorialized that Russia could redress the vulnerability of its far east by establishing friendly relations with China.[82] Baluyevskiy also linked China to Russia's need for nuclear deterrence, the implication being that China nonetheless poses a strategic threat to Russia.[83] In that same edited volume, retired Lieutenant-General A. F. Klimenko pointed to U.S. intelligence estimates that China would become the dominant military force in the region by 2025 to call for increased cooperation with China but also for the expansion of multilateral forums like the SCO.[84] This pattern, citing U.S. studies of the growing capabilities of the PLA and the threat posed by these developments, occurs often in writings by Russian military strategists and seems to be an attempt to downplay the military threat while nonetheless calling attention to it.[85] The Russian military thus seems to support a strategy of hedging its bets with regard to China, calling for cooperation in the hopes of avoiding direct military conflict and balancing against the

---

[80] Evgeniy Bazhanov, "Russian Perspectives on China's Foreign Policy and Military Development," in Jonathan D. Pollack and Richard H. Yang, eds., *In China's Shadow: Regional Perspectives on Chinese Foreign Policy and Military Development*, Santa Monica, Calif.: RAND Corporation, CF-137-CAPP, 1998, p. 82.

[81] McDermott, 2020, pp. 54–57.

[82] McDermott, 2020, p. 57.

[83] McDermott, 2020, p. 57.

[84] McDermott, 2020, p. 58.

[85] Roger N. McDermott, *Russian Perspective on Network-Centric Warfare: The Key Aim of Serdyukov's Reform*, Fort Leavenworth, Kan.: Foreign Military Studies Office, 2011, p. 14.

United States while guardedly acknowledging the military imbalance in China's favor.[86]

The analysis thus far suggests that the answer to the final question posed in this section is that the Russo-Sino partnership indirectly affects the United States and NATO in a confrontation with Russia. Russia and China do not seem poised to implement a formal alliance that would require one another to send forces in the event of a conflict. It is also unclear what forces exactly the PLA could usefully bring to the fight. The PLA Navy, for example, has relatively little experience operating outside its home waters or in antisubmarine warfare.[87] One could imagine a scenario in which Chinese forces come to Russia's aid in the event that Russian forces are being routed and pushed back into Russia.[88] This scenario lacks credibility, if only because this presents the exact type of situation Russia has declared would cause it to initiate a strategic nuclear strike.[89] In the event of a nuclear riposte by Russia to halt advancing NATO forces, it is thus difficult to see how Chinese conventional forces would be particularly relevant.

China could conceivably provide somewhat more intangible benefits to Russia, for example, by joining the latter in blocking a UN Security Council resolution intended to sanction Russia. China could thus undermine NATO efforts to isolate Russia, providing Russia with enough economic and diplomatic support to keep Russia in the confrontation longer than might otherwise be the case.[90] Theoretically, China could also leverage its central position in the global supply chain, for example, limiting shipments of medical supplies to the West. It is not clear, though, that China would view being perceived as choosing sides as in its best self-interest. After all, Russia cannot

---

[86] Richard Weitz, *Parsing Chinese-Russian Military Exercises*, Carlisle, Pa.: Strategic Studies Institute, U.S. Army War College, 2015, p. 2.

[87] Richard Weitz, "Assessing the Sino-Russian Baltic Sea Drill," *China Brief*, Vol. 17, No. 12, September 20, 2017.

[88] Interjecting Chinese forces at this point would be similar to China's actions during the Korean War.

[89] President of Russia, *Basic Principles of State Policy of the Russian Federation on Nuclear Deterrence*, Moscow: Ministry of Foreign Affairs of the Russian Federation, June 8, 2020b.

[90] Kaczmarski, Katz, and Tiilikainen, 2018, p. 60.

match the economic value of the West to China in terms of trade, technology, and investment.[91] Neutrality seems like the more probable outcome.

The potential also certainly exists that China could seek to opportunistically capitalize on such a confrontation. Yet, it is not immediately obvious whether that would come at the cost of either the United States or Russia. China could use the opportunity to aggressively pursue reunification with Taiwan. However, China could also use the Russian military's redeployment to the western front to annex its ancestral lands—and associated natural resources—in the Russian Far East. The cost and intensity of the fight is no doubt great in the former option relative to the latter option. It is thus not clear from this discussion whether reclaiming Taiwan or the Russian Far East would be the best option for China. This is not to say that either of these options is likely—Chinese neutrality might well be the most likely—but this alliance of strategic cooperation does not guarantee that Beijing will side with Russia.

One of the key assumptions of the 2008 military reforms was that the Russian armed forces would be structured to manage a military contingency primarily in one strategic direction. Future favorable relations with China (and manageable relations with Japan) will give Russia space to concentrate forces in the western strategic direction, currently the most likely region of future war.

Future War

Russian planners must make judgments on future war based on several variables. The first judgment is whether war will be rapid or protracted. Roughly speaking, rapid wars end in weeks or months with relatively few casualties; protracted wars end in years after heavy losses on both sides. Historically, if the two sides of a conflict possessed large amounts of material and human resources, the war was unlikely to terminate quickly. The second consideration is whether war will happen without much warning with peacetime forces, or there will be lead time of a building crisis that will allow for mobilization and a buildup of wartime forces. Finally, the

---

[91] Kaczmarski, Katz, and Tiilikainen, 2018, pp. 50–60.

judgment on the decisiveness of the initial period of future war is critical to determine what type of military strategy is most appropriate. Can Russia be decisively defeated by NATO in a matter of weeks or months? Could Russia defeat NATO quickly? These are the important questions that will influence other strategic decisions.

Russia's current decisionmaking process on the character of future great power war is informed by how the global and regional military-political situations (VPO, in Russian) are forecast to evolve over time. VPO forecasts include examinations of trends across foreign policy, military, sociocultural, and economic domains. States take actions across these policy areas that make war with Russia more or less likely. Those actions, particularly in the military domain, also determine the character of future war based on the probable adversary and their preferred way of warfare.[92] In the 1920s, Soviet military strategists generally agreed that war with a capitalist country in Europe was the most likely great power war scenario. The Soviet General Staff during the Cold War concluded that large-scale coalition warfare on a global scale—nuclear or conventional— should be the primary scenario for strategic planning. In turn, this led to discussions and debates about the forces that the Soviets needed to prevail in such a conflict.

In the first decade of the post-Soviet period, it was not immediately clear how the Russian Federation was going to be oriented from a political standpoint. Was Russia on a path to liberal democracy and a broader geopolitical vision in line with Western aims? Might it one day become a member of the European Union or NATO? If that were the case, planning for future war would be quite different than a situation in which Russia and another great power were pursuing opposed geopolitical outcomes. A question raised in the early 2000s during a military panel by Viktor Litovkin, a correspondent for the MoD publication *Red Star*, captured this issue at the time:

> Can anyone say what kind of state we have now? What is its orientation? It is a social state. Is it, forgive me for asking, building capitalism with a human face or socialism with a capitalist face? No one has said. No one has stated what our state's long-term objectives are. Who will

---

[92] Reach et al., 2022.

be our friends, who will oppose us, what will be the threats against us ten, 20, and 30 years from now?[93]

These questions were relevant for the Russian military in the leadup to large-scale military reforms in 2008 that were debated for well over a decade beforehand. A cadre of retired Soviet officers believed strongly that Russia needed to maintain an armed force based on mass mobilization for a future war with other great powers, such as the United States (NATO) or China, which Russia would be sure to come into conflict with at some point.[94] Additionally, proponents of this line of thinking argued that a "model of national defense based upon total mobilization" would ensure Russia's national will to fight for generations to come.[95] Others argued that even if Russia were to eventually come to blows with NATO, the character of the war would be such that mass mobilization would not be relevant.[96]

The character of modern wars in the late 20th and early 21st centuries influenced Russian thinking about future war. The transition to "non-contact warfare," conducted primarily in the aerospace domain and supported by robust digital networks—in addition to the lack of large ground formations throughout the European continent—required a force structure that was quite different from that of the Soviet period. Moreover, Moscow assessed the likelihood of large-scale war to be low based on force disposition, the level of hostile intentions of possible great power adversaries, and the condition of Russia's strategic deterrence potential relative to other nuclear states.[97]

---

[93] Jacob W. Kipp, "A Review of: 'Vladimir Slipchenko and Makhmut Gareev,'" *Journal of Slavic Military Studies*, Vol. 20, No. 1, 2007a, p. 156.

[94] Kipp, 2007a, p. 153.

[95] Jacob Kipp, "Introduction," in Makhmut Gareev and Vladimir Slipchenko, *Future War*, trans., Fort Leavenworth, Kan.: Foreign Military Studies Office, 2007b, p. vi.

[96] N. E. Makarov, "Tezisy vystupleniia nachal'nika General'nogo shtabe Vooruzhennykh Sil Rossiiskoi Federatsii—pervogo zamestitelia Ministra oborony Rossiiskoi Federatsii generala armii N. E. Makarova," *Vestnik Akademii voennykh nauk*, Vol. 1, No. 26, 2009a, p. 22.

[97] Sergei Belokon' explained in 2018 that these were the primary factors by which Russia made assessments on the likelihood of war. See, S. P. Belokon', "Otsenivanie sostoianiia natsional'noi i voennoi bezopasnosti Rossii: ustanovlennyi poriadok i vozmozhnye puti

On the basis of these military-political assessments, Russia in 2008 embarked on an overhaul of its armed forces, which Russian strategists believed would primarily be used in local conflicts along Russia's periphery. Were a war with NATO to occur, it would not be characterized by large numbers of ground forces that invaded the Russian homeland, like the Nazis in 1941. Future war in the initial period would be distinguished by long-range precision attacks by both sides against "critically important targets" in conjunction with other nonmilitary measures in the leadup to war to weaken the capability and will of the opponent to resist. This meant that Russia's Ground Forces (*sukhoputnye voiska*) would be historically small (for them), with 300,000 troops by 2020, but equipped with modern weaponry and staffed with predominantly contract soldiers.[98] The same was true for the Navy, Aerospace Forces (VKS), Airborne Troops (VDV), and Strategic Nuclear Forces (SNF).

Up until approximately 2012, there was a clear correspondence between Russian rhetoric on the character of future war and its behavior. Local conflicts were the primary planning scenario that drove Russian military strategy.[99] Strategic nuclear forces, long-range conventional strike weapons, and national air defense were the primary tools to deter conflict with NATO, China, or perhaps Japan. The General Staff largely abandoned mass mobilization and prioritized historically small, permanently ready forces that could quickly respond to and localize low-intensity armed conflicts along Russia's border. In a worst-case scenario, the initial phase of a high-intensity war with a great power would rely on strategic mobility to reinforce forces in the western or eastern strategic directions. In brief, Russia sought to replace mass with readiness and high mobility that would allow it to manage escalation with different types of adversaries.

---

sovershenstvovaniia," *Vestnik Moskovskogo gosudarstvennogo universiteta*, Seriia 25, *Mezhdunarodnye otnosheniia i mirovaia politika*, Vol. 1, 2018, pp. 30, 36.

[98] By *contract soldiers*, we mean enlisted Russian servicemembers who have voluntarily signed a contract with the Ministry of Defense to serve for a specified amount of years—a professional soldier.

[99] Samuel Charap, Dara Massicot, Miranda Priebe, Alyssa Demus, Clint Reach, Mark Stalczynski, Eugeniu Han, and Lynn E. Davis, *Russian Grand Strategy: Rhetoric and Reality*, Santa Monica, Calif.: RAND Corporation, RR-4238-A, 2021.

This approach was close to what Svechin described as a *destruction strategy*. The most likely war would be against a weaker opponent and would not be protracted. The more unlikely big war likewise was not expected to last very long because neither side was seemingly prepared in any way to wage a long war. If a regional war were to break out in Europe, there would not be time for Russia to mobilize the country because of the U.S.' ability to generate and employ air power in a "matter of hours."[100]

Over the past twelve years, the VPO has become more tense along Russia's western and southern borders, while the east is more stable given the current state of relations with China (see above section on China).[101] NATO has deployed a small number of ground forces along Russia's border in the Baltic region, as well as in Poland and Romania. Although the probability of great power war has perhaps increased in Russian assessments and forecasts (there has been no official documentation of this), the Russian expectation of NATO execution of noncontact warfare in the initial period of a future war has not changed.[102] Military strategists continue to predict that great power war up to the 2030s will be based on, at least in the initial period, the use of conventional long-range precision munitions and other advanced technologies against critical military and nonmilitary infrastructure (see Figures 2.2 and 2.3, which are dated but still generally reflective of current thinking).[103] Anti-space and cyber weapons will contribute to the mission of destroying or degrading critical enablers for warfighting (and modern life).[104] There is a bias in Russian military thought that the "civilizational

---

[100] Makarov, 2009a, p. 21.

[101] S. V. Surovikin and Iu. V. Kuleshov, "Osobennosti organizatsii upravleniia mezhvidovoi gruppirovkoi voisk (sil) v interesakh kompleksnoi bor'by s protivnikom," *Voennaia mysl'*, No. 8, 2017, pp. 5–6.

[102] V. V. Gerasimov, "Razvitie voennoi strategii v sovremennykh usloviiakh. Zadachi voennoi nauki," *Vestnik Akademii voennykh nauk*, Vol. 2, No. 67, 2019, p. 6; and Timothy Thomas, "Russian Forecasts of Future War," *Military Review*, Vol. 99, No. 3, May–June 2019.

[103] Reach et al., 2022, p. 102; Gerasimov, 2019; and I. M. Popov and M. M. Khamzatov, *Voina budushchego: kontseptsual'nye osnovy i prakticheskie vyvody*, Moscow: Kuchkovo pole, p. 415.

[104] V. M. Burenok, "Razvitie sistemy vooruzheniia i novyi oblik Vooruzhennykh sil RF," *Zashchiti i bezopasnost'*, No. 2, 2009, p. 15.

FIGURE 2.2

Russian Threat Perception and the Scale of Future War by Strategic Direction

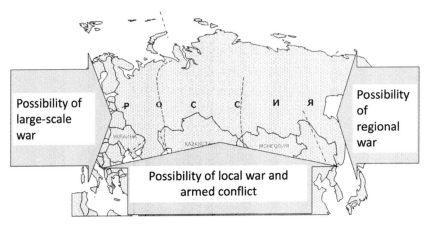

SOURCE: Burenok, 2009.
NOTE: Figure reproduced courtesy of East View Information Services.

factor" in the United States and other Western countries will pressure governments and militaries to avoid human and material losses of a contact war given their comfortable lifestyles and aversion to casualties.[105]

Given geopolitical conditions as of this writing in mid-2021, the United States and NATO are the most likely adversary for Russia in a future great power war. A Russian forecast to 2035 predicted that a smaller-scale military conflict in Ukraine or the exacerbation of territorial disputes in Poland or the Baltics could lead to a war involving both Russia and NATO.[106] There was no (public) forecast of a possible war with China over the same period.

The ability to accurately target critical infrastructure of the military and the country will affect the conduct of offensive and defensive operations in a future "systems-network war." Although the targeting of enemy force

---

[105] A. A. Bartosh, "Strategicheskaia kul'tura kak instrument voenno-politicheskogo analiza," *Voennaia mysl'*, No. 7, 2020, pp. 7–8; and V. N. Tsyigichko, "O kategorii 'sootnoshenie sil' v potentsial'nykh voennykh konfliktakh," *Voennaia mysl'*, No. 2, 2002, p. 55.

[106] Sambu Tsyrendorzhiev, "Prognoz voennykh opasnostei i ugroz Rossii," *Zashchita i bezopasnost'*, Vol. 4, 2015.

FIGURE 2.3

Character of Future Great Power War in the 2030s in the Western and Southwestern Strategic Directions

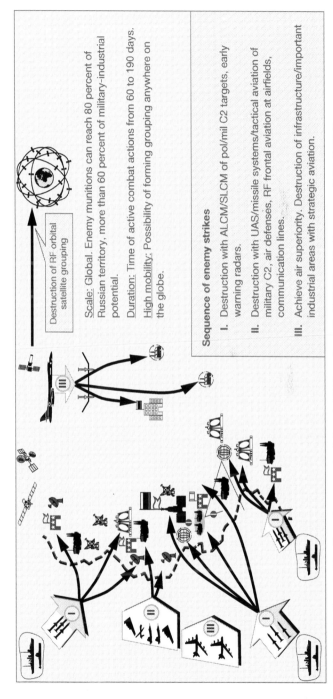

Destruction of RF orbital satellite grouping

Scale: Global. Enemy munitions can reach 80 percent of Russian territory, more than 60 percent of military-industrial potential.

Duration: Time of active combat actions from 60 to 190 days.

High mobility: Possibility of forming grouping anywhere on the globe.

Sequence of enemy strikes

I. Destruction with ALCM/SLCM of pol/mil C2 targets, early warning radars.

II. Destruction with UAS/missile systems/tactical aviation of military C2, air defenses, RF frontal aviation at airfields, communication lines.

III. Achieve air superiority. Destruction of infrastructure/important industrial areas with strategic aviation.

SOURCE: V. M. Burenok, "Razvitie systemy vooruzhenia i novyi oblik Vooruzhennykh sil RF," *Zaschita i bezopasnost'*, No. 2, 2009.
NOTE: ALCM = air-launched cruise missile; C2 = command and control; pol/mil = political/military; RF = Russian Federation; SLCM = submarine-launched cruise missile; UAS = unmanned aerial system. Image reproduced courtesy of East View Information Services.

groupings at the outset is likely to remain a part of Russian military operations into the 2030s, there have been discussions of a transition to operations that do not prioritize primary force groupings, instead focusing efforts on the underlying infrastructure that supports the precision strike system.[107] As Slipchenko wrote of future war, "It is important to mention that in next-generation warfare, starting with the sixth, man will not be the main target of a strike. He will be defeated indirectly, through the destruction of other structures and systems that support human life."[108] In 2009, Russian missile and artillery officers, whose formations now include the short-range ballistic missile Iskander brigades, described two key trends that were expected to influence operational art in the future:

> [T]here is a growing trend toward a gradual transition from fires effects against manpower to the enemy's means of destruction, reconnaissance, and command and control.
>
> The next trend, directly related to the first, is the transition from the defeat of large groups of enemy forces to the deprivation of their ability to function, the consequences of which are equivalent to defeat. In turn, this will lead to the predominance of methods of selective, functional, and structural targeting (destruction of "critically important" targets) in fire engagement, a transition from destruction of targets to disorganization of their functioning.[109]

A recap of a 2010 conference of retired senior Russian military officers reported much the same, adding important details about the creation of a new strategic operation to reflect the changes in modern warfare and the possible consolidation of strategic operations into a single, unified operation:

> In the postwar years, the operational-strategic views on the conduct of wars were revised in connection with the emergence of nuclear weap-

---

[107] Popov and Khamzatov, 2016, p. 495.

[108] V. Slipchenko, "Informatsionnyi resurs i informatsionnoe protivoborstvo," *Armeiskii sbornik*, No. 10, 2013, p. 53.

[109] V. Konstantinov and A. Stepanov, "Razvitie teorii i praktika boevogo primeneniia raketnykh voisk i artillerii v armeiskikh operatsiakh," *Zashchita i bezopasnost'*, No. 3, 2009, p. 31.

ons. [Today,] wars are characterized by a change in the priorities of fires engagement—from the destruction of the enemy to the destruction of his key targets.

The change in the character of wars is reflected in the structure of the forms of employment of the Armed Forces. A strategic operation to destroy critical targets [SODCIT] has been developed. "The era of the theory of defensive and offensive front-line, oceanic strategic operations and wartime districts is over," General Barynkin said. "It has become necessary to combine strategic defensive and offensive operations and strategic operations in the oceanic theater of operations into a unified strategic operation."[110]

In a 2019 speech on military strategy, Gerasimov offered his own views of future war that captured some of the themes highlighted in these quotes. Beginning with the possibility of an internal uprising within Russia, he highlighted U.S. developmental concepts, against critical infrastructure within Russia such as Prompt Global Strike, that in combination with domestic unrest could create a grave threat to the country. Gerasimov described the Russian response to this as "active defense."[111] Active defense is, in fact, based on "preventative [preemptive] measures for the neutralization of threats to the security of the state."[112]

We explain in Chapter Three how Russian strategic operations could fit into these preventative measures. But it is important to point out here that Russian operational concepts are apparently based on Gerasimov's scenario of future war, which considers the threat of long-range precision conventional strikes against critical infrastructure within Russian territory. In this speech, Gerasimov characterized it this way: "The policy that is being carried out by our Western partners compels us 'to respond to a threat with a threat' and plan for future strikes against the centers of command and control as well as against the sites from which cruise missiles could be launched against targets on Russian territory."[113] He added that Russia "must preempt

---

[110] Eliseeva, 2010.

[111] Gerasimov, 2019.

[112] Gerasimov, 2019.

[113] Gerasimov, 2019.

the enemy with our own preventative measures, quickly identify his weak points, and create the threat of unacceptable damage against him."[114] The identification and targeting of weak points is a continuation of a theme highlighted by the Chief of the Main Operations Directorate, General-Colonel Andrei Kartapolov, in a 2015 speech.[115]

The key takeaway from the prior discussion is that Russia is basing its views on future war on assumptions about NATO actions. The first assumption is that NATO can build up a force capable of conducting the type of destructive operations that have been observed in previous conflicts against less-capable adversaries. A previous study found that the NATO force package in and around Europe consists of thousands of aircraft and long-range munitions, several carrier strike groups, hundreds of UASs, and cruise missile submarines in both the high north and Mediterranean, among other assets.[116] How NATO manages to generate such combat power has not been explained in the Russian sources that we have consulted. Perhaps some combat power could be built up slowly in Europe over the course of years, rendering a preemptive Russian strike somewhat implausible in peacetime. Although this is a critical question for further study, for now we can say that Russia appears to believe that the forces could be mustered if required and these NATO forces could potentially achieve decisive battle against it if the appropriate Russian countermeasures are not taken. The possibility of decisive battle against Russia by NATO is the second critical assumption that has significant influence on Russian military strategy.

As a result, Russian officers are not inclined to "exhaust" the stronger power of the country's advantages and wait weeks or months for a more opportune time to launch a counteroffensive. In the late 2000s, the then–Chief of the Main Operations Directorate, Aleksandr Rukshin, advocated for a policy of "preemptive actions against an emerging threat," an issue that

---

[114] Gerasimov, 2019.

[115] Andrei Kartapolov, "Uroki voennykh konfliktov, perspektivy razvitiia sredstv i sposobov ikh vedeniia. Priamye i nepriamye deistviya v sovremennykh mezhdunarodnyh konfliktakh," *Vestnik Akademii voennykh nauk*, Vol. 2, No. 51, 2015.

[116] Clint Reach, Vikram Kalambi, and Mark Cozad, *Russian Assessments and Applications of the Correlation of Forces and Means*, Santa Monica, Calif.: RAND Corporation, RR-4235-OSD, 2020, pp. 115–130.

required thoughtful attention prior to the publication of the 2010 Military Doctrine.[117] According to Kartapolov a few years later, "the most important thing here is the principle of intensity in action, regardless of whether it is offense or defense. Passive conduct of military actions in the expectation of 'exhausting' the offensive push of the enemy will inevitably lead to the loss of control over friendly forces and, ultimately, to their defeat."[118] Gerasimov twice used the term "preventative" in his remarks on military strategy toward NATO.

Russia seems to be in the process of building an armed force and developing operational plans to maximize the effect of strikes against critical infrastructure (*weak points*) in a future war. The key component of this strategy is the *triad* of Russian long-range strike abilities—air-, sea-, and ground-launched cruise and ballistic missiles—augmented by electronic warfare, cyber, and counterspace assets (see Figure 3.2). The crucial questions for NATO are: (1) What is the trajectory of Russian capacity to execute these concepts? (2) How vulnerable is NATO to a strategy based on the prioritization of critical infrastructure (as opposed to a more-traditional counterforce approach limited to military targets)? and (3) What might the effects of these strikes be on both NATO's warfighting ability and on the populations that these strikes are intended to influence?

Conclusion

Russia's assessment of the balance of power and its forecast of future war are surprising. There is a perceived power imbalance with NATO that hypothetically could lead to a brief war in which Russia is defeated. However, this conclusion seemingly equates Russia with the former Yugoslavia and Libya. The overall balance of power is tilted toward NATO, to be sure, but Russia has a large military, expansive territory and natural resources, and an economy that, while small in comparison with leading Western countries, is still considerable. Russia could potentially draw on at least material help from

---

[117] Rukshin, 2007, p. 25.

[118] Kartapolov, 2015, p. 33.

China. Thus, the idea of a rapid, decisive defeat of Russia is not intuitive when put in the context of military history.

What could be driving Russian views of future war is a belief in the decisiveness of widespread domestic unrest within Russia combined with long-range precision guided missile attacks within Russia that undermine the regime's ability to manage control of the country. This is a very different scenario, beyond anything being contemplated in the West for the defense of NATO territory. Nevertheless, it is critical to understand because we examine trends in force structure and mobilization readiness and operational planning in the following chapter. Regardless of how the war starts, Russia will be informed by preconceived notions and the forces and plans that it has developed to counter NATO based on the scenario that is driving Russian planning.

CHAPTER THREE

Trends in Force Structure and Mobilization Readiness

Introduction

This chapter examines how Russian views on the balance of power and future war are affecting force and mobilization readiness. How Russia is prioritizing its mobilization system is of particular interest. Although the overall balance of power might suggest the need for a ready and robust mobilization system, the forecast of future war is one that Russia seems to expect could be over in a matter of six months. If the view of future war is genuine, then we would not anticipate much attention in Russian military strategy to mobilization to build up forces over time in support of a long war that far surpasses the capacity of peacetime forces and supplies.

Force Readiness

Using the forecast that says that future war is not likely to be protracted in any plausible scenario, Russia continues to prioritize readiness of peacetime forces above all. Having smaller professional forces with the modern weapons and equipment available to quickly begin operations to execute system and force destruction tasks on short notice is the driving objective (with some caveats that we address in the subsequent section).

The force structure of the Armed Forces of the Russian Federation decreased substantially from 1990 to the mid-2000s, from 4.8 million to approximately 1.3 million troops in total. The 2008 reforms reduced the total force by an additional 300,000 troops, including the reduction of the number of senior officers. The reforms reduced the authorized number of Russian military servicemembers to 1 million, organized into the reduced number of five military districts.[1] As opposed to the Soviet mass mobilization system with skeleton units, in each Russian military district there are "permanently ready units and formations" (*soedineniia i voinskie chasti postoiannoi gotovnosti*), which are supposed to be staffed exclusively with contract soldiers. These formations exist across the Russian armed forces— in fighter and helicopter aviation, air defense troops, the Ground Forces, airborne, naval infantry, and likely the fleets.[2] According to amendments made to the federal law on the status of military servicemembers, there is, in fact, a distinction made between regular contract soldiers and contract soldiers serving in permanently ready units and formations.[3] These ready units are likely Russia's "tip of the spear" in any military conflict that begins with little lead time in any immediate strategic direction (west, southwest, south, east, north).

The other important force structure trends are the partial return to maneuver divisions and the buildup of nonnuclear deterrence potential, i.e., the conventional capabilities required to inflict deterrent damage on critical military and nonmilitary infrastructure at ranges beyond that of Russian artillery (see Chapter Four). Together, these three trends are suggestive of Russian military planning for the initial period of war.

Permanent Readiness Units

In the early 1990s, Russia began to contemplate what a new military might look like based on the altered geopolitical conditions of the post–Cold War period. It would be wrong to say that the Russian military ever stopped considering NATO as a long-term military threat. There were several other

---

[1] As of 2021, Joint Strategic Command (OSK, in Russian) North is a military district.

[2] A. S. Rukshin, "Doktrinal'nye vzgliady po voprosam primeneniia i stroitel'stva Vooruzhennykh sil Rossii, *Voennaia mysl'*, No. 3, 2007, p. 27.

[3] Gosudarstvennaia duma, "Vladimir Shamanov: Priniat zakon po dopolnitel'nym meram sotsial'noi podderzhki voennosluzhashchikh," webpage, December 18, 2018. See also KonsultantPlus, "Obzor izmenenii Federalnogo zakona ot 27.05.1998 N 76-FZ 'O statuse voennosluzhashchikh,'" webpage, December 27, 2018.

overarching considerations, however. The likelihood of a large-scale war requiring state mobilization was exceedingly low. Russia did not have the economic wherewithal to maintain a large armed force. There were also questions of the suitability of universal conscription given experiences of the Soviet period. While there were clear advantages of a mobilization military for Russia, such as the ability to build up mass at relatively low cost, in 1992, Russian military and defense experts began to weigh a mixed contract-conscript force in the nonofficer ranks. The benefit would be more reliable, ready forces to move quickly in a crisis.

If the forecast were trending toward brief military conflicts of varying intensity, then greater readiness to inflict a lightning blow would make sense. A tradeoff of partial professionalization would be that a smaller, more-ready force would limit mobilization potential that could be required if great power war with NATO or China became more likely. The costs and benefits on readiness would become central flashpoints in the debate on force structure that still has not completely subsided, even if the military and political leadership seem to have decided in favor of professionalization and high readiness.[4] We detailed the central arguments of the reform leaders, who favored greater readiness over mass and mobilization, in a previous report.[5] However, we did not cover permanent readiness formations and units (hereafter, permanent readiness units), which are key components of the strategy.[6]

The 2008 reforms were an acceleration of a previously existing experiment to professionalize at least part of the enlisted ranks of the Russian military. An important law signed by Putin in 2003—"The Transition to Staffing with Military Members Serving Under Contract in Formations and Combat

---

[4] In late 2017, Putin asserted his intention that the Russian military should eventually become a fully professional force. See, "Putin zaiavil o postepennom ukhode ot sluzhby po prizyvu," *Izvestiya*, October 24, 2017.

[5] Reach, Kalambi, and Cozad, 2020, pp. 115–122.

[6] *Formations (soedineniia)* are either a division, brigade, or regiment in Russia's land forces (Ground Forces, airborne, and naval infantry) and air defense troops. *Combat units (voinskie chasti)* are battalions or companies in the land forces and air defense troops. Formations can also refer to first-t or second-order groupings of surface vessels in the Navy. We did not find discussion of the Air Force (VVS) in Russian literature on permanent readiness.

Units from 2004–2007"—laid the groundwork. The purpose of the law was to create the incentives and prestige necessary to increase the number of contract soldiers from 22,100 to 138,722 and to "improve the combat preparedness of the constant readiness formations and combat units" over the course of the four-year period.[7] The law sought to improve the contract-conscript ratio, not only in formations across the armed forces but also the Federal Security Service (FSB) Border Troops and the Internal Troops of the Ministry of Internal Affairs (VV MVD).[8] The breakdown of the plans were as follows: 125,359 military personnel; 9,729 MVD; and 3,634 FSB.[9]

Technically speaking, a permanent readiness unit should be staffed exclusively with contract personnel and prepared to begin to execute assigned missions within one hour of receiving an order. By the end of 2004, this permanent readiness qualification applied to the 76th Airborne Division (headquartered in Pskov) and the 42nd Motor Rifle Division (Chechnya), each of whose 100-percent contract staffing was the first task under the new law. From 2005 to 2007, the plan was to fill an additional 72 military formations and units exclusively with contract soldiers across the armed forces.[10] By late 2007, 19 formations and units had been converted to contract staffing (some 41,000 personnel) within the Ground Forces and Airborne Troops. Throughout the armed forces, the numbers were 62 and 93,000, respectively.[11] According to the Chief of the General Staff, Nikolai Makarov, 17 percent of the combat units in the Russian military could be considered "permanently ready" as of mid-2009.[12] By 2010, according to the plan of the time, Russia intended to increase to 60 permanently ready

---

[7] Government of Russia, "O federal'noi tselevoi programme 'Perekhod k komplektova-niiu voennosluzhashchimi, prokhodiashchimi voennuiu sluzhbu po kontraktu, riada soedinenii i voinskikh chastei' na 2004-2007 gody," No. 523, August 25, 2003.

[8] It is difficult to confirm—based on the language of the law as well as other Russian military sources—whether other branches, such as the Navy and combat arms, were a part of this initial reform effort.

[9] Government of Russia, 2003.

[10] Yurii Baluevskii, "Opiraias' na dostignutoe—idti dal'she i uverenee," *Rossiiskoe voennoe obozrenie*, No. 1, 2006, p. 4.

[11] "FTsP: Podvedenie itogov," *Krasnaia zvezda*, October 20, 2007.

[12] Nikolai Makarov, "Armiia XXI veka," *Voenno-promyshlennyi kur'er*, June 17, 2009.

formations and units in the Ground Forces and convert all airborne formations to high-readiness status to serve as rapid reaction forces.[13]

Despite these changes in the preceding three-and-one-half years, there
were a number of readiness issues identified during the 2008 war with Georgia: among these were C2 breakdowns and the ability to conduct operations
at night.[14] The 2008 military reforms nevertheless doubled down on the shift
toward permanent readiness. In fact, 70 percent of the entire armed force was
to be permanently ready. By 2020, all formations and combat units would
be fully staffed and equipped at wartime levels, 70 percent of the arms and
equipment within these elements would be "modern," and 100 percent of the
nonofficer personnel would be serving on contract in the formations and
combat units, which would be prepared to move to execute assigned tasks
within one hour.[15] In the Ground Forces, for example, all of the combined
arms maneuver brigades would meet these requirements; this was intended
to give Russia the ability to match or exceed NATO's Response Force.[16]

If Makarov, in his position as Chief of the General Staff, was present-
ing the grand vision, others further down the ranks had to deal with the
technicalities. In 2010, Colonel Valerii Maskin, who served within the Main
Operations Directorate and the TsSVI GSh, pointed out that the reality of
daily life in the military simply did not allow for such widespread combat
readiness. After annotating a number of reasons—ranging from the capacity of the military-industrial complex to the length of time it takes for servicemembers to get from their domicile to their equipment—Maskin proposed various categories of permanent readiness. "Instant reaction forces"
would make up 30 percent of the general-purpose forces and be prepared to

---

[13] "Evolutsiia kontrakta: 2007 god," *Rossiiskoe voennoe obozrenie*, No. 6, June 2007,
p. 51.

[14] Reach, Kilambi, and Cozad, 2020, p. 117.

[15] "Doklad ministra oborony Rossiiskoi Federatsii na rasshirennom zasedanii kollegii
Ministerstva oborony Rossiiskoi Federatsii 'Ob itogakh deiatel'nosti Ministerstva obo-
rony Rossiiskoi Federatsii v 2008 godu s uchetom rezul'tatov finansovo-ekonomicheskoi
raboty i zadachakh na 2009 god," *Na strazha Zapoliar'ia*, No. 23, March 21, 2009; and
V. Borsin and E. Bei, "Tema OGP dlia ofitserov '100-letie sozdaniia Krasnoi Armii,'"
Armeiskii sbornik, No. 2, February 2018, p. 55.

[16] V. M. Maskin, "K voprosu o soderzhanii soedinenii i voinskikh chastei v kategorii
postoiannoi gotovnosti," *Voennaia mysl'*, No. 1, 2010, pp. 26–27.

execute assigned tasks in less than ten hours. Rapid-reaction forces would make up another 30 percent of formations and combat units and be ready in 48 hours or less. The remaining 40 percent were augmenting forces who would have 30 days to get to the fight after weapons and equipment requiring maintenance and other certifications could be ready for combat. The final category included mobilization forces, which would be available one year or less after the outbreak of hostilities.[17]

It is difficult to determine the extent to which the aforementioned ideas were formally put into practice. Maskin's concerns nevertheless have been justified by practice in some cases. As of 2021, the Russian military is not the permanently ready force that was envisioned by the reforms, which were perhaps overly ambitious by design.[18] In 2014, 40,000 conscripts drafted in the spring for service in the Western Military District "[were] completing their training based on specialty . . . and in the near future would be sent to constant readiness formations and combat units to continue their military service."[19] Technically speaking, conscripts are not supposed to deploy and participate in conflict zones outside Russian territory. Since 2015, the number of conscripts across the entire armed has decreased by around 30,000. This, along with other evidence, suggests that there are still many permanently ready formations that do not meet the proposed requirements.[20]

One of the primary issues in properly staffing permanently ready units has been the lag in Russian recruitment (and possibly retention) of contract soldiers. Initially, there was a plan to increase the number of professional soldiers across the armed forces to 499,000 by 2020. By 2013, the target

---

[17] Maskin, 2010, p. 29.

[18] In Russian legislation on the status and treatment of military servicemembers, there is a distinction made for those formations and combat units that have been transitioned to exclusively contract staffing, which suggests that there are others that have not. See Government of Russia, "O statuse voennosluzhashchikh," Federal Law No. 76-FZ, December 8, 2020d.

[19] "Vesti," *Krasnaia zvezda*, August 2, 2014.

[20] A. V. Khomutov, "O reshenii problem primeneniia obshchevoiskovykh formirovanii takticheskogo zvena v sovremennykh voennykh konfliktakh," *Voennaia mysl'*, No. 6, 2020.

number had dropped to 425,000. The new future goal is 475,600 by the end of 2025.[21] From 2016 to 2020, the total number of contract soldiers hovered around 384,000, while the number of conscripts has been fairly steady: around 265,000 draftees per year.[22]

The Aerospace Forces and Navy

Within the Navy and VKS, we have yet to uncover much discussion of permanent readiness units. This remains a key gap in our research that we hope to address in a future study. What we can say is that the VKS has received the greatest prioritization among the service branches in allocations for weapons and equipment modernization.[23] From roughly 2009–2020, the VKS received approximately 70 battalions of the SA-21 SAM system and approximately 500 combat aircraft.[24] Russian personnel policy was supposed to be synchronized with weapons modernization. In theory, VKS units should be at least 70 percent contract personnel as of 2020.[25]

The lack of robust modernization of the strategic bomber force and military transport aviation were key gaps that contradict Russian military strategy.[26] Difficulties in development of the perspective PAK DA long-range bomber led to a mid-course correction in 2015 to instead focus on modernization of the Tu-160. The Tu-160M2 is not expected to enter service until at least 2023, with a total of 50 expected to be delivered over the next decade.[27]

---

[21] Gil Barndollar, "The Best or Worst of Both Worlds?" blog post, Center for Strategic and International Studies, September 23, 2020.

[22] Based on presidential decrees that are published for the spring and fall draft cycles.

[23] Richard Connolly and Mathieu Boulègue, *Russia's New State Armament Programme: Implications for the Russian Armed Forces and Military Capabilities to 2027*, London: Chatham House, Royal Institute of International Affairs, 2018, p. 8.

[24] Centre for Analysis of Strategies and Technologies, "Postavki boevykh samoletov v Voorzhennye Sily v 2019 godu," blog post, LiveJournal, January 16, 2020; and Kollektsioner Baionov, "Postavki sistem protivovozdushnoi oborony v Vooruzhennye Sily Rossii v 2020 g." blog post, LiveJournal, January 9, 2021.

[25] Connolly and Boulègue, 2018, p. 8.

[26] Julian Cooper, *The Russian State Armament Programme, 2018–2027*, Rome: NATO Defense College Research Division, Russian Studies, May 2018, p. 6.

[27] Cooper, 2018, p. 6.

As of late 2017, there were a total of 60 long-range bombers in the long-range aviation (LRA) fleet.[28] Current delays have left Russia with an aging and relatively limited bomber fleet, a portion of which are the primary platforms for Russia's conventional ALCMs. Russia's military transport aviation aircraft have similarly experienced several production delays over the past decade.[29] Were Russian rail communications to be significantly disrupted, a lack of a second option to move forces could be consequential in a future conflict.

Overall, however, the limited information that is available suggests that the air force and air defense forces of the VKS could be in a state of relatively high readiness; this assumption is based on the probable high number of professional forces and modernized weapons systems. At the same time, more research is required to better understand whether or how increased investment in this service branch has translated into higher readiness to execute critical offensive and defensive operations in a high-intensity conflict in Europe.

There is a small amount of evidence that first- and second-rank ships were a component for the Navy's permanently ready forces.[30] A first-rank ship, according to Russian classification standards, is 5,000 tons or more and has a mission of blue-water presence and warfighting, either independently or as part of a larger formation. Cruisers and destroyers, among others, apply to this category. Submarines carrying long-range cruise missiles to target industrial or administrative centers are also classified as first-rank.[31] The project 885 Yasen class cruise missile submarine is one exam-

---

[28] "Dal'niaia aviatsiia VKS RF. Dos'e," TASS, December 22, 2017.

[29] Aleksandr Stukalin, "K voprosu o sovremennom sostoyanii Voenno-transportnoi aviatsii v Rossii," *Eksport vooruzhenii*, Vol. 33, No. 5, September–October 2017, pp. 57–63; and Ben Connable, Abby Doll, Alyssa Demus, Dara Massicot, Clint Reach, Anthony Atler, William Mackenzie, Matthew Povlock, Lauren Skrabala, *Russia's Limit of Advance: Analysis of Russian Ground Force Deployment Capabilities and Limitations*, Santa Monica, Calif.: RAND Corporation, RR-2563-A, 2020, pp. 17–18.

[30] Mikhail Khodarenok, "Voennye reform ispytyvaiut defitsit novatorstva. Organizatsionno-shtatnye meropriiatiia v Vooruzhennykh silakh dvizhutsia po zamknutomu krugu," *Nezavisimoe voennoe obozrenie*, July 20, 2001.

[31] Aleksandr Shishkin, "Klassifikatsiia boevykh korablei VMF RF," blog post, Live-Journal, May 23, 2015.

ple. A second-rank ship has a displacement from 1,500 to 5,000 tons, which allows it to operate in open seas or world oceans. In decades past, permanent readiness ships and submarines were supposed to be able to deploy in 24 hours. At that time, because of limited fuel availability and other supplies, readiness timelines shifted to 120 hours.[32]

Return of Divisions

One of the most significant changes to Russian force structure over the past decade has been the return of maneuver divisions in the Ground Forces. Russia, if plans do not change, will have formed eight motor rifle divisions and two tank divisions between 2013 and 2023. In terms of military districts, four would be established in the western, two in the southern, one in the central, and three in the eastern. It is important to note, however, that these "new" formations were actually created on the basis of existing brigades. This makes it more difficult to gauge the net increase in combat power. Table 3.1 shows the alterations the Ground Forces formations over time. Table 3.2 shows the overall personnel numbers since 2015 and offers

TABLE 3.1

Combined Arms Formations, 2018 and 2025, Planned

	Western	Southern	Central	Eastern
Divisions, 2018	3	1	1	1
Divisions, 2025	4	4	1	1
Brigades, 2018	5	9	9	11
Brigades, 2025	4	3	6	9

SOURCE: Igor Shevtsov, "Perspektivy razvitiia sukhoputnykh voisk i voenno-morskogo flota VS RF na sovremennom etape," Moscow: Military Training Center of the Ground Forces—Combined Arms Academy of the Armed Forces of the Russian Federation, 2018; Diana Mikhailova, "Osobennosti novykh divizii sukhoputnykh voisk Rossii. Chast' 1" blog post, November 7, 2018.

---

[32] Khodarenok, 2001.

TABLE 3.2

Overall Military Personnel Numbers, 2015–2020

	2015	2016	2017	2018	2019	2020
Officers	198,000	*205,000*	*205,000*	*205,000*	*205,000*	205,000
Warrant officers	53,000	*53,000*	*53,000*	*53,000*	*53,000*	*53,000*
Contract soldiers	352,000	384,000	374,000	384,000	394,000	384,000
Conscripts	297,000	307,000	276,000	260,500	267,000	263,000
Authorized total	980,000	N/A	1,013,628	1,013,628	1,013,628	1,013,628
Active-duty total	900,000	949,000	908,000	902,500	919,000	905,000

SOURCE: Prokhor Tebin, "O chislennosti Vooruzhennykh sil RF," blog post, LiveJournal, December 12, 2015; Ministry of Defense of the Russian Federation, "Vystuplenie Ministra oborony Rossiiskoi Federatsii generala armii Sergeia Shoigu na rasshirennom zasedanii Kollegii Minoborony Rossii," December 22, 2016; President of Russia, "O prizyve v aprele – iiule 2016 g. grazhdan Rossiiskoi Federatsii na voennuiu sluzhbu i ob uvol'nenii s voennoi sluzhby grazhdan, prokhodiashchikh voennuiu sluzhbu po prizyvu," Order No. 139, March 31, 2016a; President of Russia, "O prizyve v oktiabre – dekabre 2016 g. grazhdan Rossiiskoi Federatsii na voennuiu sluzhbu i ob uvol'nenii s voennoi sluzhby grazhdan, prokhodiashchikh voennuiu sluzhbu po prizyvu," Order No. 503, October 3, 2016b; President of Russia, "O prizyve v aprele – iiule 2017 g. grazhdan Rossiiskoi Federatsii na voennuiu sluzhbu i ob uvol'nenii s voennoi sluzhby grazhdan, prokhodiashchikh voennuiu sluzhbu po prizyvu," Order No. 135, March 31, 2017a; President of Russia, "O prizyve v oktiabre – dekabre 2017 g. grazhdan Rossiiskoi Federatsii na voennuiu sluzhbu i ob uvol'nenii s voennoi sluzhby grazhdan, prokhodiashchikh voennuiu sluzhbu po prizyvu," Order No. 445, September 29, 2017b; President of Russia, "O prizyve v aprele – iiule 2018 g. grazhdan Rossiiskoi Federatsii na voennuiu sluzhbu i ob uvol'nenii s voennoi sluzhby grazhdan, prokhodiashchikh voennuiu sluzhbu po prizyvu," Order No. 129, April 2, 2018a; President of Russia, "O prizyve v oktiabre – dekabre 2018 g. grazhdan Rossiiskoi Federatsii na voennuiu sluzhbu i ob uvol'nenii s voennoi sluzhby grazhdan, prokhodiashchikh voennuiu sluzhbu po prizyvu," Order No. 552, September 28, 2018b; President of Russia, "O prizyve v aprele – iiule 2019 g. grazhdan Rossiiskoi Federatsii na voennuiu sluzhbu i ob uvol'nenii s voennoi sluzhby grazhdan, prokhodiashchikh voennuiu sluzhbu po prizyvu," Order No. 135, April 1, 2019a; President of Russia, "O prizyve v oktiabre – dekabre 2019 g. grazhdan Rossiiskoi Federatsii na voennuiu sluzhbu i ob uvol'nenii s voennoi sluzhby grazhdan, prokhodiashchikh voennuiu sluzhbu po prizyvu," Order No. 472, October 2, 2019b; President of Russia, "O prizyve v aprele – iiule 2020 g. grazhdan Rossiiskoi Federatsii na voennuiu sluzhbu i ob uvol'nenii s voennoi sluzhby grazhdan, prokhodiashchikh voennuiu sluzhbu po prizyvu," Order No. 232, March 30, 2020a; President of Russia, "O prizyve v oktiabre – dekabre 2020 g. grazhdan Rossiiskoi Federatsii na voennuiu sluzhbu i ob uvol'nenii s voennoi sluzhby grazhdan, prokhodiashchikh voennuiu sluzhbu po prizyvu," Order No. 581, October 1, 2020c; Iulia Kozak, "Pravo stat' zashchitnikom rodiny," *Krasnaia zvezda*, October 2, 2017; Aleksei Savelov, "Chislennost' voennosluzhashchikh po kontraktu v Rossiiskoi armii vozrosla bolee chem v dva raza," *Tvzvezda.ru*, November 6, 2018; Sergei Shoigu, "Armiia Rossii kardinal'no obnovlena," *Krasnaia zvezda*, March 13, 2019; Ministry of Defense of the Russian Federation, "Strategicheskie yaderniye sili," presentation, undated-c; President of Russia, "Ob ustanovlenii shtatnoi chislennosti Vooruzhennykh sil Rossiiskoi Federatsii," Order No. 555, November 17, 2017c.

NOTE: Italics are estimates, which are based on publicly reported officer numbers from 2015 and 2020 and reported warrant officer numbers from 2015.

a data point in the question of the net increase in combat power—Russian troop numbers remained steady from 2015 to 2020 despite the increase in the number of divisions.

The return to divisions and the continued reliance on battalion tactical groups (BTGs) raise questions on future war. Motor rifle divisions, depending on their configuration, have approximately twice the personnel of brigades, more than three times the number of tanks, and substantially more artillery. They can cover broader fronts and are generally more useful for seizing and holding larger swaths of territory. Perhaps the terrain of eastern Europe along Russia's border lends itself to divisions in the eyes of Russian planners, who also had other reasons for partially transitioning back to divisions. But divisions are slower to deploy because of their larger size and require more personnel to deploy at full strength. BTGs can form quickly and move to where they need to go. And because there are not prepared defenses of large formations anywhere across from Russia, these nimbler but smaller forces are not necessarily at risk of being overwhelmed initially. Given the historically small number of divisions thus far established within the Russian Ground Forces, it does not appear that a major shift in Russian thinking on the character of great power future war has occurred. At the same time, the motor rifle and tank divisions within the 1st Guards Tank Army would be a critical component of any offensive or defensive land operations along Russia's western border.

Procurement within the land forces does not suggest any major realignment in Russian thinking about future great power war and operations. The 2027 State Armaments Program is a continuation of modernization efforts that were begun in earnest in 2011. The Ground Forces have secured a greater portion of the procurement budget at the expense of the Navy, which suggests that Russia did reassess its prioritization for the following decade of military weapons and equipment investment. The VKS, which includes air forces, air and missile defense, and space forces, will continue to be the largest recipient of weapons procurement funding.

Despite the consensus on the character of future war and an overall emphasis on readiness of peacetime forces, Russian planners are also considering the possibility that initial trade of fires strikes might not be decisive. In previous conflicts in Iraq (2003), the former Yugoslavia (1999), and Libya (2011), the United States and its allies were able to achieve strategic political objectives in the course of weeks because the opposing side proved incapable of weathering the initial blow. Importantly for understanding the Russian perspective, the head of state was removed from power and killed or died in prison as a result of the aforementioned military conflicts. In Libya, Muammar Qaddafi was not apprehended by invading forces but by domestic opposition forces. This outcome reportedly had some impact on Putin's thinking toward the West.[33]

According to a Russian military expert, Russia has the means to disrupt noncontact warfare and the decisive initial strikes, which could move the war beyond the initial period.[34] Although Russian military thought tends to emphasize the centrality of the initial period, there are signs that Russia is hedging for the possibility of a longer war that lasts longer than previous military conflicts in which the United States and its allies took part. One example is the recent Russian effort to improve its mobilization system.

Russian Mobilization Activities

The military reforms of 2008 transitioned Russia's armed forces from being based on mass mobilization to being built on permanent readiness. The reasoning was that, if an adversary like the United States could build up sufficient combat power in a short period of time to launch devastating long-range strikes to critical military and nonmilitary infrastructure across Russian territory, there simply would not be time to mobilize large numbers of forces. Although Russia did not do away with state and military mobilization, sustainment and improvement was not prioritized in military planning. The armed forces could draw on former conscripts and limited contract servicemembers, who were obliged to join the reserves for a period of time, but they were not considered operationally ready. They likely would

---

[33] Evan Osnos, David Remnick, and Joshua Yaffa, "Trump, Putin, and the New Cold War," *New Yorker*, February 24, 2017.

[34] Vasilii Burenok, "Oruzhie sudnogo dnia," *Zashchita i bezopasnost'*, Vol. 2, No 85, 2018b, pp. 8–9.

need to go through several months of training prior to entering combat.[35] In other words, Russia was placing a heavy premium on the decisiveness of the initial period of war, essentially ruling out the idea of a protracted war. In isolation, this pointed to a strategy of destruction in any type of military conflict, which placed less emphasis on mobilization using a forecast of a quick war.

Reprioritization of Mobilization

In early 2013, the newly appointed defense minister, Sergei Shoigu, delivered a speech before the Russian Academy of Sciences. He presented a list of priorities for his tenure. He had a broad agenda with many unsurprising elements, such as modernizing weapon systems and improving the military C2 system. But Shoigu referenced mobilization in two of his priorities, which included the "development of the mobilization base."[36] For a large country like Russia—one that has been invaded on numerous occasions and with large military powers to its west and east—it was perhaps inevitable that it would not allow its mobilization system to be ignored indefinitely. At the same time, the prioritization of the system was a departure from a forecast that future great power war would be a brief affair. It was also curious for the local conflicts along Russia's periphery that the previous military leadership had considered most likely. Would even a historically small Russian military of 700,000 total service members and a ground force of approximately 150,000 (as of 2013) need to be augmented by the mobilization base to fight in Georgia, Ukraine, Belarus, or Central Asia? Would Russia need to call on the mobilization base to suppress widespread domestic unrest, the other threat considered likely by Russian leadership? Mobilization in the context of local conflicts on the periphery was a partial rejection of the principle of permanent readiness formations that was at the foundation of the military reforms.

---

[35] This is based on comments by a Combined Arms Academy professor on how long conscripts have to serve prior to being sent into combat. See Khomutov, 2020.

[36] S. K. Shoigu, "Vystuplenie ministra oborny Rossiiskoi Federatsii generala armii S. K. Shoigu," *Vestnik Akademii voennykh nauk*, Vol. 1, No. 42, 2013, p. 7.

Despite the ambiguity, in 2013, President Putin approved a new provision (*polozhenie*) for the General Staff within the "On Defense" law that gave greater authority to the Russian General Staff to coordinate mobilization activities. This authority was related to training not only the armed forces but security and executive organizations that would be involved in a nationwide defense effort in large-scale war. The descriptions of the provision by the Chief of the General Staff in 2014 and 2015 left the impression that Russia was perhaps taking more seriously its preparations for a protracted great power war—a war that Russian official documents and statements asserted was unlikely. Speaking in 2015 of the ongoing changes to the organization of national defense, Gerasimov stated:

> The experience of developing the Defense Plan of the Russian Federation has shown the need for clear legislative regulation of joint activities of federal executive bodies. Indeed, in the event of a real threat to the security of our country, already in the threatened period, all federal departments, their territorial bodies, [and] regional and local authorities are included in the process of organizing defense.
>
> Moreover, for the implementation of defense goals, resources and nonstate structures of all forms of ownership will be involved—enterprises, fuel and energy companies, [and] transport. It should be emphasized that all movements and concentration of resources must be synchronized with the developed plans for the use of the Armed Forces.
>
> Therefore, one of the most important tasks of the General Staff today is to coordinate the activities of military command and control bodies and state authorities in working out the preparation and implementation of measures for the transfer of the Armed Forces, other troops, [and] military formations and bodies to the organization and composition of wartime.[37]

These remarks, which included the nationalization of industry, resources, and energy supplies in wartime, painted a much different picture than that of Gerasimov's predecessor, Makarov. Makarov argued in 2009 that

---

[37] V. V. Gerasimov, "Opyt strategicheskogo rukovodstva v velikoi otechestvennoi voiny i organizatsiia edinogo upravleniia oboronoi strany v sovremennykh usloviiakh," *Vestnik Akademii voennykh nauk*, Vol. 2, No. 51, 2015, p. 14.

Preempting the enemy in the deployment of troops, success in the first battles and engagements will play a significant—if not decisive—role in the course or outcome of the war as a whole. Thus, our Armed Forces and the economic sector of the state will probably not be presented with any "threatened period" for carrying out mobilization measures. This circumstance dictates the need to have a combat-ready, trained and equipped armed forces.[38]

Makarov was bringing together several components of strategy to promote destruction over attrition in future great power war. Gerasimov was swinging the pendulum back at least somewhat toward protracted conflict. Perhaps the new leadership believed that the 2008 reforms had gone too far.

Ready Reserves

On paper, Russia possesses a large pool of reserves that could be called up during the special period in the leadup to a likely war—approximately 2 million people who served in the military between 2015 and 2019.[39] These reserves are supposed to bring existing formations and units up to full strength and to form new ones on the basis of new peacetime mobilization deployment centers (see following section).[40] Some Russian military experts, however, were calling attention to a lack of strategic reserves early on under Shoigu and Gerasimov. Referencing the Makarov-era reforms, General-Lieutenant Vladimir Ostankov explained in 2014 that the mixed contract-conscript force structure did not create, in his view, a sufficient mobilization base of ready reserves. The decision that led to this situation "was justified not only from the point of view of the mobilization tension of the state, but also from the military-strategic point of view, since it was not planned to use

---

[38] Makarov, 2009, p. 22.

[39] International Institute for Strategic Studies, *Military Balance*, Vol. 120, London: Routledge, 2020.

[40] Bogdan Stepovoi, Aleksei Ramm, and Evgenii Andreev, "V rezerv po kontraktu," *Izvestiya*, February 13, 2018.

the RF [Russian Federation] Armed Forces in large-scale military conflicts and deploy numerous groupings of troops (forces) for this."[41]

The mobilization base concerns stem from several factors. First, contract soldiers serving for multiple years decrease the annual numbers of military-trained people entering into the reserves. Second, once a conscript leaves military service, they return to civilian life with skills and fitness that degrade over time. Because released conscripts do not train or engage in perhaps any physical activity, they cannot be considered ready.

In late December 2012, Russia added a section on reserves within the law "On Military Obligations and Military Service." This new section created a reserve (*zapas*) for the armed forces, the Foreign Intelligence Service (SVR), and the FSB. Former personnel from these entities who do not formally conclude a contract to perform periodic military duties make up the *mobilization pool (mobilizatsionnyi liudskoi resurs)*.[42] The *mobilization reserve (mobilizatsionnyi liudskoi rezerv)* includes those who have signed a contract to participate in the reserve, which involves "training for military service upon mobilization and the execution of obligations of military service" in specific situations.[43] The training for the military reportedly involves two or three days per month and one 20- to 30-day training session per year.[44] By 2015, Russia planned to have recruited up to 9,000 individuals to be reservists committed to the armed forces.[45]

---

[41] V. I. Ostankov, "Strategicheskikh rezervov net," *Voenno-promyshlennyi kur'er*, March 17, 2014.

[42] This arrangement was long contemplated by Russian military analysts who foresaw the challenges that were created in the mobilization system by transitioning to a contract-conscript force structure in the nonofficer ranks. See Val'demar Fedorov and Aleksandr Tereshchenko, "Voennaia reforma: problemy i suzhdeniia. Armiia sil'na rezervom," *Krasnaia zvezda*, October 3, 1997; and V. V. Smirnov, "Kontraktnaia armiia v Rossii: problemy i puti ikh reshenii," *Voennaia mysl'*, No. 2, February 2003, pp. 2–7.

[43] President of Russia, "O vnesenii izmenenii v otdel'nye zakonodatel'nye akty Rossiiskoi Federatsii po voprosam sozdaniia mobilizatsionnogo liudskogo rezerva," Federal Law No. 288-FZ, December 30, 2012b.

[44] Stepovoi, Ramm, and Andreev, 2018.

[45] "Chislennost' mobilizatsionnogo rezerva VS RF sostavit poriadka 9 tysiach," RIA Novosti, March 14, 2013.

Since the appearance of the new reserve section in the 2012 law, several related documents have been approved at the legislative and executive levels. The following year, for example, the Russian government passed a statute updating existing law on reserve training. In mid-2015, Putin signed a decree (No. 370) that established an updated mobilization reserve that would be part of an experiment with "a new system of training and the buildup of people eligible for mobilization."[46] Because Russia already had established a mobilization reserve on paper, this new presidential decree was evidence that the previous system was unsatisfactory in some way. Perhaps there were problems in attracting the 9,000 personnel mentioned in the initial target. The 2015 decree directed that federal budget funds be made available to the Ministry of Defense for activities related to formation of the mobilization reserve, which was tested in the Tsentr-2015 strategic exercise.[47]

Because the 2008 reforms did away with many of the previous elements of the mobilization system—skeleton units and a predominantly conscript service—it was not clear exactly how Russia would mobilize reservists, who those reservists would be, and where they would serve. The 2015 decree was the launching point toward resolving some of these questions, but there were again delays. At least one test took place in Rostov oblast' (along Russia's southwestern border with Ukraine); it involved signing contracts with reservists to train on a monthly basis. However, a full-fledged, country-wide effort to implement the program envisaged by the 2015 decree did not begin until early 2018. The Vostok-2018 strategic exercise included some reserve units.[48] This might have been a test of activation of parts of the mobilization reserve that had been built up to that point.

All reservists are assigned either directly to a military unit or to a *mobilization deployment center*: These centers are supposed to replace the previous storage and repair bases. The storage and repair bases were reportedly staffed with only ten people apiece, and they were not able to manage the

---

[46] President of Russia, "O sozdanii mobilizatsionnogo liudskogo rezerva Vooruzhennykh Sil Rossiiskoi Federatsii," Order No. 370, July 17, 2015.

[47] Iulia Kozak, "Prizyv vo imia bezopasnosti otechestva," *Krasnaia zvezda*, October 24, 2018.

[48] Kozak, 2018.

upkeep and maintenance of the weapons and equipment at the bases.[49] In 2016, a new mobilization center was built in Sakhalin that could house and equip a unit the size of a motor rifle battalion (approximately 500 soldiers and associated weapons and equipment).[50]

In sum, Shoigu and Gerasimov are in the very initial phases of building a hedge against a great power war of longer duration. At the same time, the emphasis on readiness of the reserves suggests that Russia is still concerned about the need to mobilize additional forces quickly. What we can conclude from the legal and readiness changes is that Russian leadership believes that it might need to call on reserves, a portion of whom need to be ready to fight at the outset, while the rest of the mobilization system also needs to be prepared to support a war that could last longer than a few weeks. However, the effort to address the readiness portion of the mobilization system only began in earnest in 2018. Russia, as with the war forecasts shown in Figures 3.1 and 3.2, could be looking toward the early 2030s with regard to the development of a long war hedge.

Territorial Defense

Legal provisions on territorial defense were expanded and more explicitly detailed in 2013. Prior to the 2013 amendments, "On Defense" stated only that territorial defense "is organized in order to protect the population, facilities and communications on the territory of the Russian Federation from enemy actions, acts of sabotage or terrorist acts, as well as the introduction and maintenance of states of emergency and martial law" and that the president determines the tasks and organization.[51] Although there were other updates to the Territorial Defense section, Gerasimov highlighted an additional clause that allowed for the declaration of martial law and conduct of territorial defense within specific boundaries of Russia. According to the new clause,

> Territorial defense shall be conducted on the territory of the Russian
> Federation or in its individual localities where martial law has been

---

[49] Stepovoi, Ramm, and Andreev, 2018.

[50] Stepovoi, Ramm, and Andreev, 2018.

[51] President of Russia, "Ob oborone," Federal Law No. 61-FZ, December 30, 2012c.

introduced, taking into account the measures applied during the period of martial law.[52]

Interagency territorial defense headquarters (HQs) that would function during periods of martial law were also established by the law. The executive leadership of the constituent entities bears personal responsibility for functioning of the territorial defense HQs, according to the law. One of the explicit tasks of the HQs is to ensure the efficient coordination of territorial defense, civil defense, mobilization, and counterterrorism activities within their areas of responsibility, which are determined using the geographical boundaries of the 85 subjects of the Russian Federation (including Sevastopol and the Republic of Crimea, which are not internationally recognized).[53]

Within each military district, there are territorial defense groupings (organized by subjects within the military district) under the control of the aforementioned HQs that consist of military and internal security troops.[54] As of 2014, one Russian analyst estimated that there were perhaps between 60,000 and 100,000 personnel within each military district who were designated for territorial defense tasks, or up to 400,000 in total for the east, west, central, and southern military districts.[55]

Russia's cultivation of territorial defense forces appears puzzling on its face because of a seeming mismatch between these forces and the conflicts for which the Kremlin is preparing. Without a serious prospect of a foreign ground invasion, why emphasize territorial defense? As discussed previously on the topic of future war, most Russian analysts envision con-

---

[52] President of Russia, "O vnesenii izmenenii v otdel'nye zakonodatel'nye akty Rossiiskoi Federatsii," 55-FZ, April 5, 2013. See also V. V. Gerasimov, "Rol' General'nogo shtabe v organizatsii oborony strany v sootvetstvii s novym polozheniem o General'nom shtabe, utverzhdennym prezidenta Rossiiskoi Federatsii," *Vestnik Akademii voennykh nauk*, Vol. 1, No. 46, 2014, p. 16.

[53] President of Russia, 2013; and Vladimir Ostankov, "Voiny budushchego nachinaiutsia segodnia," *Voenno-promyshlennyi kur'er*, October 15, 2019.

[54] A. M. Kashcheev, Iu. A. Malinovskii, and A. M. Sazonov, "Regional'nye tsentry upravleniia sub"ektov Rossiiskoi Federatsii v sistema upravleniia territorial'noi oboronoi," *Vestnik Akademii voennykh nauk*, Vol. 1, No. 70, 2020, pp. 76–77.

[55] Konstantin Sivkov, "Kazachestvo kak novyi rod voisk," *Voenno-promyshlennyi kur'er*, March 10, 2014.

flict with NATO as a *noncontact* war whose decisive phase will be waged at great distances using precision munitions. This decisive phase is expected to be relatively brief, lasting weeks or a few months at most. It is not clear what role territorial defense would play in a war where the immediate threat comes not from invading foreign troops but high-tech weapons.

In a regional conflict against a neighboring country, such as Ukraine, Russian forces would presumably be on the offensive. Georgia and Ukraine are unlikely to attempt large-scale ground incursions into Russian territory. The role of territorial defense in an armed conflict, such as the wars in the Caucasus in the 1990s, is self-evident, but it seems that these kinds of challenges only pose serious threats in certain areas of the Russian Federation. Why, then, develop territorial defense forces across the whole of Russian territory? Admittedly, given its huge ground forces, China could pose a real threat of invading lightly defended territory in the Russian Far East.

When placed in the context of Russian leaders' threat perceptions and strategic outlook, territorial defense is arguably more sensible. Kremlin officials do not assume that any of the aforementioned war scenarios are mutually exclusive—indeed, one of their foremost fears is that powerful adversaries will cultivate multiple kinds of threats at the same time. The foremost objective of Russian strategy at all levels is regime survival. The experiences of 1917 and 1991 have taught Russian thinkers that, even in the context of an all-out great power war, the most profound threats to a government come from within. Andrei Kokoshin described the way the First World War affected the Tsarist regime:

> As the war went on and the losses mounted and the failures compounded . . . the state of Russian society was transformed. It became a truly "revolutionary situation" . . . In case of defeat, war entails the loss of society's spiritual, moral, and ethical compass.[56]

The Russian government needs comprehensive mechanisms to avoid societal breakdown under the stresses of interstate conflict. Territorial defense comprises a large part of these mechanisms.

---

[56] Andrei Kokoshin, "Neskol'ko izmerenii voiny," *Voprosy filosofii*, No. 8, 2016, pp. 15–16.

Russian leaders do not appear to assume that their country will manage to emerge from a great power war unscathed even under the best of circumstances. Indeed, their usual assumption about a conflict with NATO is that it will open with a swift, brutal, and intense bombardment with precision conventional weapons against key Russian military assets and possibly civilian infrastructure. Nor do Russian leaders ignore prospective retaliation to whatever attacks Russia might inflict on its adversaries in such a war. The belief is not that Western leaders will lack the resolve to retaliate in kind for Russian limited nuclear use or nonnuclear strategic attacks; indeed, Russian analysts appear to expect some sort of proportional retaliation.[57] The expectation seems to be that such an attack would transform the conflict to render less disadvantageous for Russia. The theory is not that Russia will experience less damage from the exchange of blows—if anything, given Russian strategists' generous estimates of Western conventional might and their overestimation of NATO willingness and capability for LNU, they probably expect to come off considerably for the worse—but that Western publics will have less toleration for such damage than Russians.[58]

Therefore, even if Russia managed to avoid outright defeat in the opening phase of a war with NATO, it would still experience extreme domestic stresses that could persist for an extended period of time even if open hostilities did not. Russian military and civilian infrastructure might be devastated and the civilian economy severely weakened. Food and potable water could be inadequate throughout much of the country, including in the largest cities. After the two world wars, it took many years for Russia to recover from analogous conditions, and in both cases multiple insurrections challenged the authority of the central government. Similar to their Soviet predecessors, contemporary Russian leaders believe that foreign adversaries will cultivate and support such domestic threats as these. Russian leaders must also reckon with the possibility of an extended crisis preceding or following hostilities. Even if the war itself proves brief, the crisis leading to it

---

[57] A. V. Fenenko, "Faktor takticheskogo iadernogo oruzhiia v mirovoi politike," *Vestnik Moskovskogo universiteta. Seriia 25, Mezhdunarodnaia otnosheniia i mirovaia politika*, No. 2, 2012; and A. V. Zagorskii, "Iadernoe oruzhiia v Evropa: vokrug status-kvo," *Kontury global'noi transformatsii: politika, ekonomika, pravo*, Vol. 11, No. 6, 2018.

[58] Burenok and Pechatnov, 2011.

might emerge many months before it, and dire domestic conditions could linger.

Nor can Russian leaders assume that a serious war with one of its post-Soviet neighbors would not cause domestic dislocations. By historical standards, Russian ground forces are quite modest in size, and the still-underdeveloped reserves system will not be able to bolster those forces substantially until some indeterminate point in the future. Nor can Moscow devote all of its available military forces to a local conflict—some would need to be available to address other threats. So even a war with a country like Ukraine could severely strain Russian resources as it dragged on, even if Russia handily defeated that country's forces in pitched battle. The almost inevitable need for a large-scale occupation force to conduct interminable counterinsurgency operations that could easily last for years would place strains on the Russian military and mobilization system that neither are currently well-equipped to meet. Territorial defense forces could make up at least some of this gap and allow a larger proportion of regular military forces to contribute to such a campaign. History provides examples of how, even with its combination of a planned economy privileging defense needs and huge mobilization reserves, the Soviet Union experienced serious internal problems from conflicts with its smaller neighbors. The 1939–1940 Winter War with Finland, for instance, caused major disruptions to the Soviet civilian economy.[59] And given the increasing technological sophistication of bordering countries' militaries, Russian leaders cannot assume that the territory will be safe from attack. Ukraine, for instance, is developing its own operational-tactical systems akin to the Russian Iskander.[60] Taken together, these considerations suggest that territorial defense forces could play a direct or indirect role in a local war.

---

[59] Elena Osokina, *Za fasadom "sotsialisticheskogo izobiliia": Raspredelenie i rynok v snabzhenii naseleniiav gody industrializatsii*, 1927–1941, 2nd ed., Moscow, 2008, pp. 272–287.

[60] "KB 'Iuzhnoe' izgotovilo opytnyi ekzemliar OTRK 'Grom-2 ['Iuzhnoe' Design Bureau Builds Prototype Example of 'Grom-2' Missile System],'" *Novosti VPK*, April 23, 2019.

TABLE 3.3

Trends in Russian Rhetoric and Actions

Strategy Component	Destruction	Transition	Attrition
Balance of power	+		
Future war	+		
Mobilization activities		+	
Force structure trends	+		
Diplomatic actions	+		
Organization of operations	?		?

NOTE: Russian assessments and forecasts of the balance of power might suggest trends toward an attrition strategy, but we show in the following section that Russian military leaders and analysts reject that approach.

Conclusion

Russia's mobilization and territorial defense activities since 2013 are trending toward greater emphasis on preparedness, although some programs appear to be in relatively nascent form as of 2021. Russia seems to be hedging against the possibility of a future war that allows for mobilization activities and lasts longer than just a few weeks as well as some other scenarios discussed in the prior section. Russian actions are also intended to allow the system to move more quickly by building up greater numbers of ready reserves who are training regularly on a monthly basis. This suggests the following Russian views on future war (see also Table 3.3):

- Future great power war might ultimately be longer than anticipated under the previous General Staff leadership.
- Russia does not believe that ready peacetime forces will be sufficient for operations in a future great power war.
- Russia believes that future war could involve some form of occupation, subversive activities, or post-war crisis that would require participation of domestic territorial defense units.

Summary of Chapters Two and Three

The summary of the preceding two parts of the report is as follows:

- Russia is the overall weaker side in the conflict.
- Russia has consolidated friendly relations with China, which allows Moscow to direct its attention and resources primarily to the west and southwest.
- Into the 2030s, the West will rely on long-range precision strikes against military and nonmilitary targets, both forward and rear, in the initial period of a war, which might not allow for much time to draw on the mobilization pool. When combined with widespread domestic unrest, these military actions could be decisive enough to undermine the regime's control of the country.
- Russia prioritizes forces that are at a high readiness level and have ample means within their formations and combat units and, under current plans through 2027, will continue to build readiness through weapons modernization and greater numbers of contract troops.
- Much hinges on Russia's ability to recruit and sustain contract personnel.
- Since 2015, Russia has been attempting to stand up a mobilization reserve comprising civilians who are obliged to train regularly throughout the year.

During the Makarov era, Russia sought to build a force more suited for destruction in the initial period of war. To be sure, Russian assessments found that local wars along its periphery were the most probable and large-scale war was unlikely. A destructive strategy against vastly weaker neighbors with conventional militaries is sensible. Russian strategy toward NATO, should deterrence fail, was probably best understood as destructive through the use of tactical and, if required, strategic nuclear weapons in the initial period of war. Russia simply had no other means to attack distant NATO forces with conventional strike. This gap would have made any defensive strategy to attrit or exhaust NATO forces, means, or both extremely difficult because of the range deficiencies of territorial air defenses in the early

2010s and the lack of a capability either to respond in kind in Europe or the United States or to disrupt the enablers of a conventional aerospace attack.[61]

Shoigu and Gerasimov have taken actions that generally align with the thrust of the previous leadership, but they have moved the pendulum slightly back toward preparing for a larger and longer war that could become protracted. These efforts, however, are only in the initial phases, leaving Russia largely structured for destruction, although not necessarily of the "main grouping of NATO [land] forces" as was the primary objective of destruction through the Soviet strategic offensive during the Cold War.

Chapter Four of the report will attempt to marry these components of Russian military strategy with Russian operational concepts to begin to shape an understanding of Russian strategic actions in a potential NATO-Russia war.

---

[61] At least some Russian planners were looking to the late 2020s or early 2030s (not the mid-2010s) in their thinking on the character of future war in the western strategic direction.

Organization of Operations—from Destruction to Contact War

As of 2021, NATO is the most likely adversary for Russia in a future great power war. Russian diplomatic actions have allowed the Kremlin to commit relatively few resources to defend Siberia and the Russian Far East against a China threat. The Russian armed forces thus have two primary tasks in the western strategic direction.[1] The first is to build a force that can deter war in Europe. The second task is to execute the war against an alliance that is forecast to possess three to five times the military potential of Russia by 2040.[2]

In this chapter, we examine the Russian organization of operations for large-scale war that will encompass most of Europe from the outset and likely expand to the world oceans and North America. There is a long history of Russian military planning using the strategic operation as the organizational concept for war planning. Strategic operations are, first of all, guided by broad principles of warfare that we examine at the outset to better understand what modern strategic operations will seek to achieve in a large-scale war. We will then discuss how the Russian General Staff and expert community is approaching the organization of operations in modern conditions, which are characterized by historically small force groupings for both Russia and NATO that are spread far from each other geographically in Europe and beyond.

---

[1] In this case, *western strategic direction* is shorthand for the entire swath of territory from the Arctic to the Caucasus.

[2] Reach et al., 2022.

Guiding Principles in the Organization of Operations

Preference for Destruction in the Initial Period of War

The evidence presented in this section and in prior ones suggests that despite overall weakness, Russian planners feel compelled to use ready forces and means to pursue sufficient destruction in the initial period of war. In a 2019 speech on military strategy (referenced previously), Gerasimov advocated targeting NATO military sites preemptively, likely in anticipation of NATO attack (or in response to such an attack, depending on the perspective).[3]

Some leading experts from across Russia's military science community similarly found that taking defensive actions in the initial period of war was an inappropriate strategy despite a negative correlation of forces. In a 2018 book on the future development of Russian force structure, the authors wrote:

> In most strategic areas, the balance of forces is not in favor of the [Russian Federation] Armed Forces by at least two [or] three times, but in some areas by more. Consequently, the assignment by experts of a correlation of forces to successfully execute defensive operations in the initial period of the war is futile.[4]

These views do not align neatly with the factors that typically influence destruction or attrition thinking. A negative correlation of forces, particularly in key warfighting categories, does not intuitively lead to a destruction strategy. All available evidence suggests that Russia does not possess an advantage in conventional long-range munitions.[5] Russia's air and naval forces similarly are neither quantitively nor qualitatively superior. We there-

---

[3] Gerasimov, 2019.

[4] Burenok, 2018b, p. 181.

[5] Fredrik Westerlund and Susanne Oxenstierna, eds., *Russian Military Capability in a Ten-Year Perspective—2019*, Stockholm: Swedish Defence Research Agency, FOI-R--4758--SE, December 2019, pp. 36–38. Between 2020 and 2024, the Department of Defense plans to acquire 170,000 precision-guided munitions (PGMs) of varying ranges. See John R. Hoehn, "Defense Primer: U.S. Precision-Guided Munitions," Washington, D.C.: Congressional Research Service, IF11353, updated June 4, 2021.

fore might expect that Russia would focus on attrition of NATO advantages through defensive operations in the initial period of war despite the risks. But the rhetorical and practical indicators point toward destruction, regardless of whether Russia is on offense or defense, with plans to mobilize reserve forces if the war drags on.

Senior Russian officers often refer to the use of asymmetric and indirect actions in their discourse on warfighting. Such actions could take many forms, from the disruption of the sociocultural situation to the "instigation of man-made disasters."[6] Russian analysts in the early 2010s promoted countervalue targeting with long-range PGMs until a larger inventory could be built, while strategic nonnuclear weapons would fill the capacity gap for counterforce targets:

> [T]he use of counterforce deterrence criteria [i.e., strikes against military targets] in the prenuclear phases of [the war] is not possible until the combat capabilities of [Russian] general-purpose forces are comparable to those of potential adversaries. In this regard, it is necessary to consider the possibility of creating asymmetric threats. As such a threat, it is necessary to consider the threat of destruction of the economic potential and critical military facilities of a potential enemy.[7]

Regardless of the ratio of symmetric to asymmetric actions that Russia conducts, one of the guiding principles will be to direct destructive actions through strategic operations to impose a way of war on NATO that is more advantageous to Russia (at least before the United States and its allies could mobilize land forces)—a contact war.

Noncontact to Contact War

One of the guiding principles in Russian operational planning against NATO is centered on moving a war from noncontact to contact. This idea dates back to at least 2003, when then–defense minister Sergei Ivanov presented a detailed list of future planning objectives for the MoD. He stated:

---

[6] Surovikin and Kuleshov, 2017, p. 8.

[7] Burenok and Pechatnov, 2011, p. 100.

The importance of creating sufficiently strong and well protected groups of land forces that will be able not only to repel enemy attacks after suffering massive air strikes, but also to immediately launch (possibly in autonomous units or groups) offensive operations in direct contact with the land troops of the enemy, will grow. We must turn the noncontact war into a contact one at the initial stage, as a contact war is what the enemy armed with long-range precision-guided weapons wants to avoid.[8]

Since that time, the idea has persisted in Russian military thought.[9] In 2010, Sergei Tashlykov, a professor of military strategy at the General Staff Academy, argued that the most effective way to fight an opponent with a preference for noncontact is to have ground forces ready to move quickly to the offensive as the other Russian service branches disrupt the long-range actions of the adversary.[10] Sergei Chekinov and Sergei Bogdanov, noted Russian military theorists, included the use of aviation, multiple rocket launchers, and electronic warfare as means to force contact on the enemy.[11] Aleksandr Serzhantov, the deputy head of the TsSVI GSh, in a 2019 interview on the future development of Russian military art, stressed the importance of imposing contact on an adversary who is inclined to avoid it.[12] If the use of permanently ready ground forces is one way to make contact with the enemy, there is another task that Russia believes must occur either prior to or in conjunction—countering network-centric warfare. The disruption of critical command, control, communications, computers, intelligence, surveillance, and recon-

---

[8] Sergei Ivanov, "The Priority Tasks of the Development of the Armed Forces of the Russian Federation, Ministry of Defense of the Russian Federation, 2003, pp. 9–10.

[9] Iu. A. Dashkin, "Problemy moral'no-psikhologicheskogo obespecheniia i puti ikh resheniia," *Vestnik Akademii voennykh nauk*, Vol. 2, No. 27, 2009, p. 40; and Burenok, 2018a, p. 8.

[10] S. L. Tashlykov, "Obshchie cherty i nekotorye osobennosti soderzhaniia sovremennykh voennykh konfliktov s uchastiem SShA i ikh soiuznikov," *Voennaia mysl'*, No. 8, 2010, p. 27.

[11] S. G. Chekinov and S. A. Bogdanov, "Evolutsiia sushchnosti i soderzhaniia poniatiia 'voina' v XXI stoletii," *Voennaia mysl'*, No. 1, 2017, p. 37.

[12] A. A. Serzhantov, interview, "Tendentsii razvitiia voennogo iskusstva," *Nezavisimoe voennoe obozrenie*, October 4, 2019.

naissance (C4ISR) linkages theoretically could force NATO to reject noncontact warfare and resort to a way of war in which Russia believes it would have an advantage.[13]

Countering Network-Centric Warfare

Russian military experts argue that it should not just be the primary assets involved in the aerospace campaign—aircraft, air bases, aircraft carriers—that should be targeted to deprive NATO of its ability to conduct noncontact warfare. The entire integrated system required for such a campaign's execution is perhaps even more important. Although Russia has its own plans to eventually employ a pared-down version of noncontact warfare that is intended for certain missions or scenarios, prominent Russian military theorists observe that automation and information transfer for the sake of it would not imbue superiority over one's adversary.[14] Absent an ability to create a network-centric army capable of outpacing the enemy's ability to observe, orient, decide and act, Russia could emphasize forces, systems, and means to asymmetrically engage the adversary by attacking the enablers of network-centric warfare, such as air- and space-based intelligence, surveillance, and reconnaissance (ISR) platforms and C2 nodes.[15] This early awareness that Russia might not be able to "achieve superiority over the enemy instead of trying to catch up with it" provides the foundation for subsequent efforts to develop alternative methods of achieving superiority.[16]

Informed by the analysis of future war, a crucial tool in the kit has been an emphasis on capabilities for electronic warfare (EW) (*radioelektronnaia bor'ba*, REB). The objective since the early 1990s, as Mary C. FitzGerald argued, has been to devise "technical and operational counters to the new technologies of "airspace war.""[17] Viewed as an asymmetric "force multiplier," Russia's emphasis on the EW assets centers around disorganizing

---

[13] Burenok, 2018a, pp. 8–9.

[14] McDermott, 2011, p. 18.

[15] McDermott, 2011, p. 18, emphasis added.

[16] McDermott, 2011, p. 18.

[17] Mary C. FitzGerald, "The Russian Military's Strategy for 'Sixth Generation' Warfare," *Orbis*, Vol. 38, No. 3, Summer 1994, p. 457.

an adversary and causing chaos by attacking its enablers of the network—situational awareness, C2, and precision—*and* protecting its own enablers.[18]

Russia's modern EW capabilities suppress and permanently damage adversary network-warfare capabilities. Russia reintroduced anti-radiation missiles into its forces and EW systems on land, sea, and air (manned and unmanned) to jam satellite and aircraft communications and navigation systems and suppress GPS signals to unmanned vehicles.[19] Russian EW forces target an expansive list of assets, including radars, antennas, space-based reconnaissance, and other sensors, as well as the structures that *interact* with these electronic systems, such as computers, data storage and their energy supply.[20] Lazukin, Korolyov, and Pavlov write that, "EW forces and assets (troops) will directly participate in fulfilling tactical tasks by ground forces formations in order to disorganize adversary troop and weapon command and control."[21] Russian Major General Yuriy Lastochkin, who is in charge of the REB force, argues that EW forces will "decide the fate of all military operations" in future wars, given that the primary goal of EW is to degrade, deny, disrupt, and destroy the enemy's ability to command and control its forces, conduct persistent ISR, and effectively employ its weapons.[22]

By denying an adversary the use of its radars, communications, reconnaissance assets, and other electronic systems across as many frequencies as possible, precision stand-off forces can be rendered less effective.[23] Therefore, in the perpetual race to hit one's adversary while avoiding being hit, EW assets

---

[18] V. F. Lazukin, I. I. Korolyov, and V. N. Pavlov, "On Basic Elements of Electronic Warfare Forces Tactics," *Voyennaia mysl'*, No. 4, 2017.

[19] Jonas Kjellén, *Russian Electronic Warfare: The Role of Electronic Warfare in the Russian Armed Forces*, Stockholm: Swedish Defence Research Agency, FOI-R--4625--SE, 2018, pp. 43–60.

[20] Kjellén, 2018, p. 26.

[21] Lazukin, Korolyov, and Pavlov, 2017, p. 30.

[22] Aleksandr Stepanov, "They Have Deployed a Dome, Which Defends from Missiles, over the Russian Bases in Syria. Unique Electronic Warfare Systems, Which Are Capable of 'Blinding' Any Precision-Guided Weapon, Provide It," *MK Online*, interview with Major-General Lastochkin, April 15, 2018.

[23] Jānis Bērziņš, "The Theory and Practice of New Generation Warfare: The Case of Ukraine and Syria," *Journal of Slavic Military Studies*, Vol. 33, No. 3, 2020, p. 365.

provide a means to increase the survivability of one's own troops, assets and infrastructure.[24] Thus, perhaps one of the more underappreciated roles of EW forces is the protection of Russia's vast aerospace defense architecture. Russia has invested heavily in air defenses whose primary purpose is to protect strategic assets located within Russia. The ground-based air defense of the VKS, which deploys the S-300, S-350, S-400, and air defense fighter aircraft, has longer range, is less mobile, and is thus not intended to operate in a contested or occupied territory.[25] EW assets identify emissions that could reveal the location of a military object and mask those emissions, thus increasing protection from anti-aircraft, aviation-related, and missile attacks.[26]

Information warfare provides the integrating layer for these nonstrategic deterrence elements—precision strike, EW, and air defense. A single, integrated information space connects and supplies data between sensors and electronic-fire assets; thus, C4ISR serves as the central nervous system for network-centric warfare.[27] Because network-centric warfare relies on information technologies, information assumes its own type of warfare, attacking the assets that provide information and using information as a social and political weapon.[28] Colonel V. N. Dybov (retired) and Colonel Yu. D. Podgornykh (retired) argue that military forces can be subject to a variety of attack vectors in the information sphere:

> Information factors include malicious software, potential presence of computer hackers; unreliable experts; information sources or basic data that have been obtained for subsequently assessing the situation and justifying the decisions made; lack of the required basic data for estimating the situation and justifying the decisions taken; the pres-

---

[24] Bērziņš, 2020, p. 365.

[25] Michael Kofman, "Russian A2/AD: It is Not Overrated, Just Poorly Understood," blog post, Russian Military Analysis, January 25, 2020.

[26] Kjellén, 2018, pp. 38–39, 84.

[27] Gerasimov, 2019, pp. 4–6.

[28] Timothy L. Thomas, "Information Weapons: Russia's Nonnuclear Strategic Weapon of Choice," *Cyber Defense Review*, Vol. 5, No. 2, Summer 2020, p. 126.

ence of false, distorted, or obsolete information in the information field; and so on.[29]

Russian military strategists suggest additional ways for information to be weaponized, including destroying, distorting, and stealing data files, data-mining files that are obtained through cyber intrusions, denying access to authorized users, causing technical equipment to malfunction, and disabling communications and computer networks that support society and state functioning.[30] Precision weapon systems similarly depend on information systems—particularly navigation and reconnaissance—to function effectively. By spoofing, jamming, dazzling, destroying, or corrupting these sources of information, Russia can decrease the effectiveness and increase the costs to U.S. and NATO forces of their preferred means of warfare. Russian military specialists discuss the value of information-strike operations with the aim of "disorganizing an adversary's troop and weapons command and control systems and destroying his information resources."[31]

System of Strategic Actions

Based on the aforementioned principles, Russia is attempting to build a force to quickly respond to a crisis in which great power war appears a likely outcome. These forces are organized into joint strategic commands (in wartime), which jointly are intended to conduct strategic operations in the initial period of a great power war, which could at an early phase, involve much of the European continent and the Arctic region. Soviet and Russian mili-

---

[29] V. N. Dybov and Yu. D. Podgornykh, "Aerospace Defense Stability in the Russian Federation," *Military Thought*, No. 4, 2019, p. 29.

[30] S. V. Markov, "O nekotoryk podkhodakh k opredeleniyu sushchnosti informatsion-nogo oruzhiya [Several Approaches to the Determination of the Essence of the Information Weapon]," *Bezopasnost*, No. 1–2, 1996, p. 53.

[31] I. N. Chibisov and V. A. Vodkin, "The Information-Strike Operation," *Armeyskii sbornik*, March 2011, p. 46.

tary strategic operations have long fallen under a broader framework known as the *system of strategic actions* (see Table 4.1).[32]

These actions are intended to deter war first of all, and then prepare the armed forces and the country to wage military conflicts of varying scales. What has changed since this framework was first presented by Makhmut Gareev in 2004 is that Russian military leadership has generally embraced the idea that there will be less time to move from peace to war, which requires both ready active and reserve forces as well as a mobilization system that can function effectively enough to deliver at least some forces to the front lines in a minimal amount of time. Since 2004, Russia has added a strategic operation known as the *strategic operation to destroy critically important targets* (SODCIT). The section that follows explains strategic operations in the context of destruction in the initial period of a future war. Some of these operations might be organized in a way that resembles Figure 4.1, which brings together many of the concepts discussed previously, including countering the network with EW and other counter-space assets.

Background on Strategic Operations

Soviet strategic operations fell within three overarching concepts: strategic offensive, strategic defense, and counteroffensive. These operations were massive in scale, involving hundreds of thousands of troops who were engaged in combat along a front that, by the 1970s, increased to a length of 2,500km and a depth of 1,500km. (During World War II, some strategic operations involved well over a million soldiers.) Strategic operations in support of the strategic offensive were predominant in Soviet military strategy beginning in the 1910s and throughout the Cold War.[33] The strategic operation concept arose from the need to command the actions of multiple *fronts*, which was a new requirement as European armies continued to

---

[32] M. A. Gareev, "Problemy sovremennoi sistemy voennogo upravleniia i puti ee sovershenstvovaniia s uchetom novykh oboronnykh zadach i izmenenii kharaktera budushchikh voin," *Voennaia mysl'*, No. 5, 2004, p. 67; V. A. Zolotarev, ed., *Istoriia voiennoi strategii Rossii*, Kuchkovo pole, 2000, pp. 457–479.

[33] S. N. Mikhalev, *Voennaia strategiia. Podgotovka i vedenie voin novogo i noveishego vremeni*, Kuchkovo pole, 2003, pp. 785–823.

TABLE 4.1

System of Strategic Actions of the Armed Forces of the Russian Federation, as of 2004

I. Strategic Deterrence

Maintain required combat capability and combat and mobilization readiness of armed forces	Maintain (strengthen) through military means diplomatic, economic, information, and other actions to assure defense; demonstrate military presence and military force	Peacekeeping actions and operations	Actions to aid troops and formations of Interior Ministry, Border Guards, and Emergency Ministry to suppress internal conflicts, protect and defend borders, and manage emergency situations	Intelligence, counterintelligence, and information actions; military cooperation with other countries	Air defense and protection of state borders in air, land, and sea domains through military means

II. Strategic Deployment of Forces

Transition armed forces from peacetime to wartime (martial law) (mobilization deployment)	Operational deployment of troops (forces) within the theater of military operations (TVD), maritime, and space domains	Deployment of first-echelon strategic reserves	Strategic repositioning of forces

Table 4.1—Continued

III. Combat Employment of Russian Federation Armed Forces in Local Wars and Military Conflicts

Combat actions of border and covering forces	Combat actions (operations) of the primary forces of border military districts	Combat actions of the Air Force in support of troops (forces) and to repel air attack	Combat actions and operations of naval forces	Limited (selective) use of nuclear weapons by SNF

IV. Strategic Operations and Actions in Large-Scale War

Strategic aerospace operation	Strategic nuclear forces operation	Strategic operation in the military theater	Strategic actions and operations of the naval forces in maritime TVD
• Special Purpose Air Army • Air Force and Air Defense Formation • Military District, fleets • Missile Defense Army • Space assets • Specialized troop formations	• Strategic rocket forces, LRA, air units with operational-tactical nuclear weapons • SSBNs, subs with SLCM (Navy) • Specialized troop formations	• Military District • Combined Arms Armies, supreme command reserve • Special Purpose Air Army • Air and Air Defense Army • Fleets • Coalition formations • Airborne formations • Specialized troop formations	• Fleets in coordination with Air Force, military districts and other branches of Armed Forces

SOURCE: Gareev, 2004.
NOTE: SSBN = ballistic missile nuclear submarine.

FIGURE 4.1

Possible Russian Military Actions in Future War in the Early 2030s

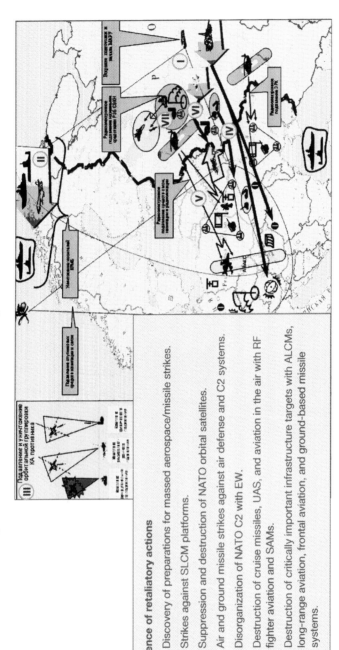

Sequence of retaliatory actions

I. Discovery of preparations for massed aerospace/missile strikes.

II. Strikes against SLCM platforms.

III. Suppression and destruction of NATO orbital satellites.

IV. Air and ground missile strikes against air defense and C2 systems.

V. Disorganization of NATO C2 with EW.

VI. Destruction of cruise missiles, UAS, and aviation in the air with RF fighter aviation and SAMs.

VII. Destruction of critically important infrastructure targets with ALCMs, long-range aviation, frontal aviation, and ground-based missile systems.

SOURCE: Burenok, 2009.

NOTE: Image reproduced courtesy of East View Services.

expand in size and improve their mobility.[34] The purpose of those operations was "to completely defeat the main grouping of enemy forces (consisting of 70–100 divisions)."[35] Strategic operations were to be sequential and possibly conducted in two strategic directions, i.e., west and southwest. It was critical throughout the conduct of operations that national air defenses provided sufficient forward breathing space for air and ground forces to execute assigned tasks and cover critical political and military-economic infrastructure in the rear, a broad tasking that required large numbers of long-range SAM systems and fighter-interceptors.

The appearance of nuclear weapons in the 1950s radically changed Soviet thinking on operations. Notably, the reaction to the impact of nuclear weapons at the time aligns very closely with Russian observations of the impact of long-range conventional munitions and noncontact warfare today:

> In the mid-1960s, in the face of the dramatic change in understanding of the character of a possible war, views on the methods of strategic actions of the Armed Forces were radically revised . . . The economy, the state administrative system, strategic nuclear means, and the aggressor's armed forces all became fully accessible for nuclear missiles, and therefore could be destroyed in a short time not only to the full depth of the theater of military operations but also beyond it.

> Strategic missile forces, strategic aviation, and nuclear missile submarines began to acquire capabilities to complete the main war tasks. Nuclear weapons greatly expanded the scope of the war: From now on, war could simultaneously grip the entire territory of the states belonging to the enemy alliance, and not just theaters of operations, as was the case in the past war. . . .

> In such conditions, there was no need to divide strategic actions into strategic offensive and defensive frameworks. Now the strategic defense as such was generally excluded. It could be conducted only on an operational scale, mostly on an army scale. *Military theorists*

---

[34] Mikhalev, 2003, p. 792.

[35] Zolotarev, 2000, p. 457.

unequivocally argued that a nuclear war gave the Armed Forces a choice: either to attack or to be defeated [emphasis added].[36]

Since 2008, the forces with which to conduct strategic operations are much smaller than anything Soviet planners ever contemplated (see Table 4.2). In wartime, five joint strategic commands (OSKs) cover respective strategic directions—west, southwest, central, east, and north. Each OSK is comparable to a front in Soviet times, and, for armed conflicts and local wars, is considered a self-sufficient force grouping.[37] The OSK commander has overall operational control over the forces within the defined territorial boundaries of the OSK, although general operational plans initially might be drawn up within the Main Operations Directorate of the General Staff. In the event of a larger war along the entire western border of Russia, from St. Petersburg to Crimea, intercommunication and interoperability between OSKs and space, air, land, and sea-based ISR will become more critical.[38] Overall C2 of joint OSK operations probably will be conducted from the Combat C2 Center within the National Defense Management Center.[39] Because Russian strategic exercises involve the movement of forces from one OSK to another, individual OSKs are not necessarily envisioned by Russian planners as conducting strategic operations independently in a regional or large-scale war with NATO.[40]

---

[36] Zolatarev, 2000, p. 461.

[37] "V VS RF na vsekh strategicheskikh napravleniiakh sozdany samodostatochnye gruppirovki voisk," TASS, November 7, 2017.

[38] S. V. Iagol'nikov, "Voenno-tekhnicheskie aspekty organizatsii i vedeniia vozdushno-kosmicheskoi oborony v sovremennykh usloviiakh," *Vestnik Akademii voennykh nauk*, Vol. 2, No. 59, 2017, pp. 61–62; S. V. Iagol'nikov, "Organizatsiia vozdushno-kosmicheskoi oborony v sovremennykh usloviiakh," *Vestnik Akademii voennykh nauk*, Vol. 2, No. 55, 2016, p. 49; and I. A. Fedotov, "Napravleniia razvitiia operativno-strategicheskogo komandovaniia voennogo okruga na sovremennom etape stroitel'stva vooruzhennykh sil Rossiiskoi Federatsii," *Vestnik Akademii voennykh nauk*, Vol. 4, No. 57, 2016; and Makhmut Gareev, "Ob organizatsii voennogo upravleniia na strategicheskikh napravleniiakh," *Natsional'naia oborona*, No. 10, October 2010.

[39] Gerasimov, 2015, p. 13.

[40] Westerlund and Oxenstierna, 2019.

TABLE 4.2

Approximate Numbers of Primary Forces for Conventional Strategic Operations in the Initial Period of War in the Western Strategic Direction (as of 2019)

	Western OSK	Southern OSK	Central OSK	Total
Ground Troops	90,000	75,000	50,000	215,000
Combined Arms divisions	4	4	1	9
Combined Arms brigades	4	3	6	13
SRBM brigades (missiles)	4 (128+)	4 (96+)	1 (32+)	8 (256+)
Other standoff conventional strike munitions				1,103+
Air and air defense armies	1	1	1	3
SA-21 SAM battalions (missiles)	34 (1,088+)	11 (352+)	8 (256+)	53 (1,696+)
Tactical aircraft	175	250	100	525
Attack helicopters	100	162	60	322
Modern missile ships	10	20	0	30

SOURCES: Shevtsov, 2018; Reach, Kilambi, and Cozad, 2020; "S-400 Missile System," web page, Wikipedia, last updated July 11, 2021; Westerlund and Oxenstierna, 2019; International Institute for Strategic Studies, *Military Balance*, Vol. 121, London: Routledge, 2021.
NOTES: SRBM = short-range ballistic missile. Foreign military base in Armenia not included in Southern OSC; Iskander brigades assumed to have 16 launchers.

As of 2012, there were at least four types of strategic operations in the doctrinal documents: the strategic aerospace operation (SAO), the strategic operation in the theater of military operations (SOTMO), SODCIT, and the strategic operation of nuclear forces (SONF).[41] Strategic naval operations do

---

[41] S. V. Ruchkin, *Podkhod k vyboru pokazatelei effektivnosti porazheniia ob"ektov protivnika iadernym oruzhiem i strategicheskim neiadernym oruzhiem, XXXI Vserossiiskaia NTK*, Chast' 4, VA RVSN, Serpukhov, Russia, 2012.

not appear within this list, which is a departure from Gareev's presentation in 2004. It might be that naval actions are considered by Russian planners to play a supporting role in other strategic operations. In 2003, the Chief of the Navy's Main Staff stated in an article on modern warfare that naval operations were "an integral part of the strategic aerospace operation."[42] That would be consistent with remarks from Gerasimov stating that cruise missile launch sites—some of which are at sea—would be targeted. Naval vessels equipped with long-range PGMs are also part of SODCIT.[43]

Historically, strategic operations were linked sequentially to achieve a common objective under a single plan. How these operations might be linked and sequenced today is unclear. There is some theoretical discussion of this in Russian military literature, which we address in a subsequent section.[44] That said, one of the primary issues in regard to sequencing is the fact that it is not obvious in some cases what separates one strategic operation from another. Based on Table 4.1, SAO and SOTMO are drawing on many of the same forces and means. SODCIT almost certainly involves the use of long-range bombers that are equipped with ALCMs. The targets in SAO and SODCIT might be different, but the assets are the same and the munitions are not unlimited. In 2019, General-Major Andrei Sterlin, A. A. Protasov, and S. V. Kreidin might have been speaking to this conceptual and practical problem in a discussion of the future of the system of strategic actions:

> One of the promising options for the system of strategic actions of the [Russian Federation] Armed Forces includes two strategic operations:
>
> - Operation of the strategic deterrence forces (OSDF);
> - Operation of general-purpose forces (OGPF).
>
>
> In the long term, it must be assumed, the line between the OSDF and OGPF will merge into a single, unified strategic operation. The reasons

---

[42] Viktor Kravchenko, "Flot v sovremennoi voine," *Morskaia gazeta*, April 17, 2003.

[43] "Ofitsial'nyi otdel," *Morskoi sbornik*, No. 1, January 2013, p. 13.

[44] Michael Kofman, Anya Fink, and Jeffrey Edmonds, *Russian Strategy for Escalation Management: Evolution of Key Concepts*, Arlington, Va.: CNA, DRM-2019-U-022455-1Rev, April 2020.

for this are already visible in the ideas under consideration for updating the Russian concepts of strategic deterrence, de-escalation, and suppression of threats to military security. In the concept of strategic deterrence, strategic offensive forces in the form of strategic nonnuclear weapons have already been included in the actions of the general-purpose forces in resolving problems in local wars. Therefore, the clear separation of the strategic deterrence and general-purpose forces into the OSDF and OGPF is crumbling. In essence, this is a harbinger of further convergence toward a unified strategic operation.[45]

Despite conceptual and practical challenges, Russian operations are intended to contain and deescalate the conflict.[46] They would not be considered *strategic* by historical standards if they were limited to a relatively small geographic area. Containing the conflict to a smaller territorial area will be challenging for Russia because U.S. and NATO bases and points of entry span the entire continent of Europe, the western Mediterranean, maritime zones in the Arctic, and the United States homeland. Figure 4.1, as well as other Russian sources, show how from the outset of the war, the theater would likely span the Arctic to the Mediterranean to the Ural Mountains east of Moscow at a minimum.[47] Thus, it is most logical to examine the conduct of Russian strategic operations across a broad war theater to degrade and destroy NATO's ability to execute noncontact warfare and to impose a contact war. Such actions could set the stage for greater Russian political influence along its western border, a centuries-long political objective of the Kremlin.

We cannot say with certainty how Russia is devising strategic operations today. Analysis of a large body of literature on Russian thinking about future

---

[45] A. E. Sterlin, A. A. Protasov, and S. V. Kreidin, "Sovremennye transformatsii kontseptsii i silovykh instrumentov strategicheskogo sderzhivaniia," *Voennaia mysl'*, No. 8, 2019, p. 16; V. B. Zarudnitskii, "Faktory dostizheniia pobedy v voennykh konfliktakh budushchego," *Voennaia mysl'*, Vol. 8, 2021, p. 44; and V. G. Ivanov, A. Iu. Savitskii, and S. G. Makarov, "Bliianie voin i vooruzhennykh konfliktov na sistemu sviazi voennogo naznacheniia," in *Radiolokatsiia, navigatsiia, sviaz': Sbornik trudov XXVI Mezhdunarodnoi nauchno-tekhnicheskoi konferentsii*, Tom 2, Voronezhskii gosudarstvennoi universitet / Sozvezdie Contsern, 2020, p. 248.

[46] For more information on conflict deescalation, see Kofman, Fink, and Edmonds, 2020.

[47] Reach, Kilambi, and Cozad, 2020, p. 123.

war leads us to conclude that it is most appropriate to think of Russian military actions in large-scale war as Sterlin, Protasov, and Kreidin described *prospective thinking*—a large joint operation of the general-purpose forces, followed by operations of the strategic nuclear forces. There are many simultaneous lines of effort within the European theater that make it difficult to neatly break down strategic operations into sequenced packages. Are some long-range bombers involved in the initial SAO to destroy airbases, while others are reserved for a later phase of the war to destroy critically important targets that could create massive panic and disruptions to urban life?[48] Might it be that SOTMO, which encompasses formations from across the armed forces, is the only strategic operation that is relevant for large-scale war with NATO? There are many outstanding questions, some of which the Russians themselves are grappling with. That said, for the purpose of our analysis we will use the existing concepts of strategic operations to walk through what is shown in Figure 4.1 and discussed elsewhere in Russian military discourse.

There is no predetermined plan of strategic operations. In World War II, the circumstances of the situation dictated details of the operational plans. Notionally speaking, for a large-scale war with NATO, planning might involve a sequence that began with an SAO to target a mix of forward military targets and aerospace system enablers with an emphasis on the latter. SAO would potentially support ground actions to seize and hold territory across eastern Europe. These actions could be followed by conventional SODCIT, if required, to inflict mass damage on primarily nonmilitary infrastructure in Europe and the United States homeland.[49] The SONF might be reserved for when Russia has exhausted conventional options to terminate or deescalate the conflict.[50] This notional sequence of actions could happen in the course of weeks or months, and there could be some overlap—some critical nonmilitary infrastructure could be targeted in con-

---

[48] Burenok and Pechatnov, 2011, pp. 171–172.

[49] Nonstrategic nuclear weapons could also play a role. See Burenok and Pechatnov, 2011, p. 151.

[50] Ministry of Defense of the Russian Federation, "Strategicheskaia operatsiia iadernykh sil (SOYAS)," webpage, *Russian Military Encyclopedia*, undated-a.

junction with SAO, for example (see aforementioned comments by Sterlin, Protasov, and Kreidin).

When Andrei Kokoshin contemplated a conflict escalation ladder in a 2018 book, *Issues in the Applied Theory of War,* he drew a distinction between a large-scale conventional war that involves the destruction of critical nonmilitary infrastructure, such as chemical factories and power stations, and war that did not (see Figure 4.2, which incorporates other Russian thinking on the subject of targeting and escalation).[51] The sequence of actions in Figure 4.1 similarly reserves strikes against critically important infrastructure strikes for the final phase. This preliminarily suggests that a SODCIT with conventional weapons targeting infrastructure that supports modern life could be the final escalatory rung prior to the employment of nuclear weapons.

FIGURE 4.2

Notional Conflict Escalation Ladder

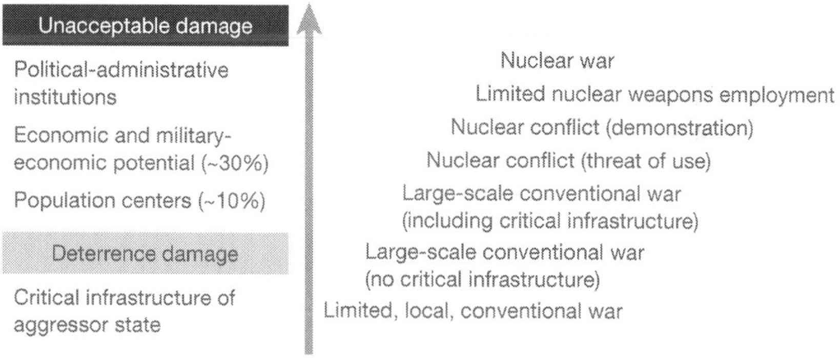

SOURCES: Kokoshin, 2018; A. G. Burutin, G. N. Vinokurov, V. M. Loborev, S. F. Pertsev, and Iu. A. Podkorytov, "Kotseptsiia nepriemlemogo ushcherba: genesis, osnovnye prichiny transformatsii, sovremennoe sostoianie," *Vooruzhenie. Politika. Konversiia,* No. 4, 2010; and Iu. A.Pechatnov, "Metodicheskii podkhod k opredeleniiu sderzhivaiushchego ushcherba s uchetom sub"ektivnykh osobennostei ego vospriiatiia veroiatnym protivnikom," *Vooruzheniia i ekonomika,* Vol. 3, 2011.

NOTE: This figure combines various authoritative Russian sources to emphasize Russian thinking on where the destruction of critical infrastructure might fit into conflict escalation. Russian authors tend to see such actions as knowingly escalatory but required because of the dire circumstances. This is a preliminary assessment on our part on the sequencing of critically important target (CIT) targeting.

---

[51] A. A. Kokoshin, *Voprosy prikladnoi teorii voiny,* Moscow: Izdatel'skii dom Vysshei shkoly ekonomiki, 2018, pp. 221–222.

Strategic Aerospace Operation

Even prior to the so-called revolution in military affairs that shifted emphasis to the aerospace domain, the achievement of air superiority in the initial period of war was crucial.[52] Without it, advantages on the ground might be diminished over time.[53] The SAO is the primary operation to achieve air superiority throughout the entire theater of war, which, initially, will include much of the European continent. This scale is what separates the SAO from the "operational-strategic" level in Russian military parlance. Operational-strategic tasks cover only one strategic direction or smaller theater of military operations.[54] There are three primary tasks of the SAO— the destruction of military targets that directly support the aerospace attack or enable it, the achievement of air superiority, and the protection of the Russian homeland.[55]

To execute SAO tasks, there are three air and air defense armies among the three OSKs that could be called on in the initial period of war to conduct an SAO in the western and southwestern strategic directions, which together probably cover most of eastern and central Europe. The east and north OSK also have air and air defense armies, although some portion of the air and air defense assets likely would be required to protect critical flanks. This would especially be the case for the territorial air defense units in the north, where NATO strategic bombers could threaten both critical naval targets and Moscow and the surrounding industrial region, a long-time concern of Soviet and Russian planners.[56]

---

[52] For the official definition and description of the SAO, see Ministry of Defense of the Russian Federation, "Strategicheskaia vozdushno-kosmicheskaia operatsiia," webpage, *Russian Military Encyclopedia*, undated-b.

[53] Jan Hoffenaar and Christopher Findlay, eds., *Military Planning for European Theatre Conflict During the Cold War: An Oral History Roundtable*, Zurich: Center for Security Studies ETH Zurich, 2007, p. 81.

[54] Mikhail Khodarenok, "Ot chego zavisit pobeda," *Vozdushno-kosmicheskaia sfera*, No. 5, 2004, p. 4.

[55] Ministry of Defense of the Russian Federation, undated-b.

[56] I. V. Erokhin, *Vozdushno-kosmicheskaia sfera i vooruzhennaia bor'ba*, Tver': Voennaia Akademiia Vozdushno-kosmichesakoi oborony, 2008, p. 232.

In keeping with the aforementioned guiding principles, the destructive component of the SAO would, in addition to launching strikes against "sites from which cruise missiles can be launched," use air-based electronic warfare and long-range strike to degrade and destroy ISR communication links.[57] In Figure 4.2, helicopter-based jammers attack AWACS aircraft, air defense, and other radar stations in central Europe. Russia has equipped most of its Sukhoi fighters and special Mi-8 helicopters with airborne jammers to disrupt targeting and missile guidance. EW forces, whose commander sits on the Russian General Staff, have been a point of emphasis in Russian thinking about ways to mitigate the strengths of a noncontact adversary, and EW has an important role in the SAO.[58] A question for a subsequent SODCIT operation is how many conventional assets are left to conduct this follow-on mission.

Another critical component of the SAO is the defense of the Russian homeland.[59] Some Russian analysts have suggested that there should be an additional operation, known as the "strategic operation to repel the enemy aerospace attack," which did exist as a concept during the Soviet period.[60] One apparent reason for adding this operation to the present system of strategic actions was that the S-400 and S-500 long-range SAM systems would allow Russian air defense forces to "independently and in conjunction with other service branches and combat arms conduct strategic tasks."[61] The author of this statement was a senior officer at the Aerospace Academy who could have been seeking greater prestige and resources for air defense

---

[57] Gerasimov, 2019.

[58] S. G. Chekinov, V. I. Makarov, and V. V. Kochergin, "Zavoevaniiu i uderzhaniiu gospodstva v vozdukhe (v vozdushno-kosmicheskoi sfere) - dostoinoe mesto v razvitii rossiiskoi voennoi teorii i podgotovke voisk (sil)," *Voennaia mysl'*, No. 2, 2017, p. 66; and I. V. Grudinin, D. G. Maiburov, and V. V. Klimov, "Strukturno-funktsional'nyi analiz protsessa otrazheniia udara stredstv vozdushno-kosmicheskogo napadeniia protivnika," *Vestnik Akademii voennykh nauk*, Vol. 3, No. 72, 2020, p. 75.

[59] Ministry of Defense of the Russian Federation, undated-b.

[60] Andrei Goncharov, "Voina budet vo vsekh sredakh," *Vozdushno-kosmicheskaia sfera*, No. 6, 2015, p. 57; D. O. Rogozin, ed., *Voina i mir v terminakh i opredeleniiakh*, Moscow: Veche, 2017, p. 155; Zolatarev, 2000, p. 464.

[61] Goncharov, 2015, p. 57.

troops. There is a long-running dispute as to whether Russia's national air defense can be effectively executed with air defense forces that are respectively subordinate to geographically bounded OSK commanders.[62] Regardless, there is no evidence that the proposal was adopted. In fact, the General Staff appears to be moving toward consolidation as opposed to expansion. Nevertheless, there is broad agreement across Russian military leadership that aerospace defense is vitally important to the deterrence and defeat of any advanced military opponent.

The organization and disposition of Russia's national air defense is centered on point and area defense of strategically important areas and facilities. The protection of forward-deployed forces is another assigned task of the VKS air defense troops, which consist of long-range SAM formations, fighter-interceptors (Su-27 and MiG-31 variants, and prospectively, the MiG-41), and radio-technical (radar) formations. Practically speaking, all Russian fighter aircraft could be used to engage with NATO aircraft.

Long-range SAM units in the west and south OSKs are primarily intended to protect critical political and military infrastructure within Russia. A secondary role for some portion of the regiments is to cover forward deployed forces. Traditionally, systems like the S-400 (SA-21) are considered national defense assets. According to retired General-Lieutenant Vadim Volkovitskii, the former Chief of the Main Staff of the Air Force, the primary task of the national air defense forces, and SAMs in particular, was to protect Russia's strategic nuclear forces bases.[63] These and other protected sites were determined by specialists who proposed a list of critical infrastructure that was ultimately approved by the president. This document is known as the "List of Critical Facilities of the Russian Federation to Be Protected by Air Defense Forces and Means" (*Perechen' vazhneishikh ob"ektov Rossiiskoi Federatsii, podlezhashchikh prikrytiiu voiskami i silami protivovozdushnoi oborony*).

---

[62] Dmitry (Dima) Adamsky, *Moscow's Aerospace Theory of Victory: Western Assumptions and Russian Reality*, Arlington, Va.: CNA, IOP-2021-U-029278-Final, February 2021, pp. 12–14.

[63] Vadim Volkovitskii, "Prikrytie strategicheskikh iadernykh sil – vazhneishaia zadacha voenno-vozdushnykh sil," *Vozdushno-kosmicheskaia sfera*, No. 6, 2009.

The list breaks down the critical facilities into four categories: state management, military, economic, and infrastructure (see Table 4.3 for an example from 1993). In the mid-1990s, there were approximately 500 facilities on the list, which were roughly divided between military and nonmilitary infrastructure. 70 percent of the sites were required to be protected directly by SAM units, while the remainder were protected "within the general air defense system by fighter aviation."[64] Subsequent cuts to the air defense forces reduced the number of facilities covered by SAM units to 380. As of 2012, there were still large gaps in coverage based on the requirements of

TABLE 4.3

Critical Infrastructure Covered by Air Defense Forces, 1993

Executive Management Facilities	Military Facilities	Economic Facilities	Infrastructure
1st category facilities	Military C2 sites	Government communications	Air transport facilities
2nd category facilities	Strategic nuclear facilities, strategic rocket forces, naval strategic nuclear forces, air strategic nuclear forces	Radioactive facilities	Sea transport facilities
3rd category facilities	Service branch and combat arms facilities	Chemical facilities	River transport facilities
	Logistics and other special sites	Atomic energy stations	Lines of communication and other infrastructure
		Hydroelectric stations	
		Regional power stations	
		Industrial centers (cities)	

SOURCE: Volkovitskii, 2009.

---

[64] Sergei Volkov, "Voiska PVO nakanune 'raskassatsii,'" *Vozdushno-kosmicheskaia sfera*, No. 2, 2006, p. 11.

SAM coverage. According to Andrei Demin, who, as of this writing, is the Commander of the 1st Air and Missile Defense Army that protects Moscow, at that time "peacetime anti-aircraft missile forces are capable of providing direct cover for no more than 59 percent of the facilities of the Armed Forces, economy, and infrastructure that must be protected by Air Defense Forces from air strikes based on the list approved by the President of the Russian Federation."[65]

Coverage has almost surely improved. From 2007 to 2020, Russian air defense forces have received 70 battalions (typically 8 launchers in each, at least 32 missiles per battalion) of the S-400 SAM system. These systems often replaced antecedents but the qualitative enhancements have improved Russia's air defense by some measure since the time Demin made his remarks in 2012.[66] Despite some independent analysis to the contrary, Russia is apparently satisfied with the current cost-benefit analysis between Russian long-range air defense systems (S-300/400/500) working against fourth- and fifth-generation aircraft.[67] However, the introduction of greater numbers of UAS swarms, such as Perdix drones, could alter that calculation.[68] As Burenok explained, "If there are hundreds of drones above the battlefield,

---

[65] Andrei Demin, "Ser'eznoi ugroze adekvatnyi otvet," *Voenno-promyshlennyi kur'er*, July 4, 2012.

[66] Volkovitskii (2009) traces in some detail the historical capability advancement of Russia's strategic SAM systems. Demin also expressed confidence in abilities of the S-400 and associated weapons and equipment to drastically improve Russia's territorial air defense coverage. See Demin, 2012.

[67] V. M. Burenok, "I grianet dron," *Voenno-promyshlennyi kur'er*, November 2, 2016. For a contrarian view that doubts that the number of air defense missiles is sufficient, see Anatolii Khramchikhin, "Voiska mirnogo neba," *Nezavisimoe voennoe obozrenie*, November 22, 2018.

[68] Russia is apparently devoting research attention to the development of explosives that can destroy certain types of low observable drones, although it is not clear that such research is specifically aimed at drone "swarms." See V. Iu. Korchak, R. V. Reulov, S. V. Stukalin, and S. A. Grigor'eva, "Nauchno-metodicheskie osnovy voenno-tekhnicheskoi otsenki nauchnykh i tekhnologicheskikh dostizhenii organizatsii Rossiiskoi Akademii nauk, vysshei shkoly i predpriiatii promyshlennosti," *Vestnik Akademii voennykh nauk*, Vol. 2, No. 55, 2016, p. 151.

using expensive SAMs against them will be like trying to smash a fly with an iPhone."[69]

Strategic Operation in the Theater of Military Operations

Doing strategic offensive operations with large groupings of ground forces had long been the central component of operational planning and military strategy. The first Gulf war and subsequent U.S.-led campaigns led some Russian military theorists to question the future role of ground forces in operations. In 2018, Vasilii Burenok, the president of the Russian Academy of Missile and Artillery Sciences, wondered whether there would even be a place for the tank on the future battlefield because of its high cost and vulnerability.[70] In most Russian discussions of future war, the initial period typically does not assign much of a role to ground forces at all on either side. In planning discussions, Russia is being attacked from the air and sea with forces who are based far from Russia's combined arms armies. Figure 4.2 is a good example in that the kinetic tasks are being carried out largely by the Russian VKS and Navy with the Ground Forces providing long-range fires from ballistic missile and EW brigades. NATO ground forces are also not pictured conducting a ground invasion of Russia or Belarus. At the same time, some Russian analysts whom we have quoted still discuss the idea of using Russia's Ground Forces to make "contact."

In the *strategic operation in a continental theater of military operations*, as it was known during the Soviet period, "the ground forces and air forces played the leading role, with participation from certain elements of the Strategic Rocket Forces (in a nuclear war), naval forces, [and] specialized troops."[71] Given that strategic operations that were exercised during the Cold War involved 80–120 divisions, in the modern era the scale of such operations is orders of magnitude smaller. As shown previously, the western, southern, and central OSKs combined have approximately 22 large maneuver formations (though not at full strength). What distinguishes SOTMO from other strategic operations is the role of the mechanized infantry for-

---

[69] Burenok, 2016.

[70] Burenok, 2018b, p. 8.

[71] Rogozin, 2017, p. 155.

mations of the ground forces, whose primary objective in the past and today was to seize and occupy territory after destroying enemy forces or to repel invading land forces.[72] The lack of prepared defenses along Russia's western border with NATO changes the nature of planning for ground operations. Russian maneuver formations could remain within Russia during the opening weeks of a conflict or essentially become occupation forces if their initial push into NATO territory is not sufficiently resisted.

The exact area of responsibility of the western OSK is not known. But it likely includes at a minimum Finland, Estonia, Latvia, Lithuania, Belarus, Poland, and a portion of northeastern Ukraine. We include Ukraine because the 20th Combined Arms Army is headquartered in Voronezh and has units scattered directly across the northern half of Russia's border with Ukraine. The immediate theater, excluding Finland, therefore comprises at least 775,000 square km of territory, approximately 60 million people, and around 100,000 land troops, including three joint NATO battalions and one U.S. armored brigade combat team. To cover this immediate area, the western OSK commander has a total maneuver force of four motor rifle divisions, one tank division, three airborne divisions, three motor rifle brigades, and one tank brigade. In all, Russia has perhaps 120,000 land forces in the western OSK, including naval infantry and VDV. Russia's permanently ready land units could include approximately 40 BTGs (28,000 troops, using the figure of 700 per BTG) and some smaller number of FSB border troops and National Guard units.[73]

Much research has been done over the course of several years into Russia's ability to seize NATO territory in eastern Europe. The current correlation of forces has created little doubt among observers that Russia's land forces are capable of creating a lot of problems for NATO in the initial period of war. Less attention has been devoted to what might come next for the invading Russian land forces; that is, holding the territory. The occupation of territory historically has been a primary objective of SOTMO or other

---

[72] Zolotarev, 2000, p. 463.

[73] For a detailed analysis of the correlation of forces in the region, see, Scott Boston, Michael Johnson, Nathan Beauchamp-Mustafaga, and Yvonne K. Crane, *Assessing the Conventional Force Imbalance in Europe: Implications for Countering Russian Local Superiority*, Santa Monica, Calif.: RAND Corporation, RR-2402, 2018.

Russian land-based operations. Indeed, 500,000 Soviet troops invaded and occupied Estonia, Latvia, and Lithuania in 1939 and 1940.[74] If it is the case that Russian forces can move quickly into a swath of NATO territory where there are not adequately prepared defenses, they will then need to transition to occupation unless some political agreement can be reached, an outcome that is unlikely and not expected by the Russian military. The management of a restive population increases the internal security requirements (the establishment of checkpoints, patrols, counterinsurgency operations) that are in addition to the external requirements of preparing for the NATO counterattack. The RAND Corporation conducted a detailed analysis of the potential internal and external security requirements of Russian land forces (including the National Guard) to seize and hold a large swath of territory in two Baltic countries—along the lines of SOTMO, in modern conditions.[75] The requirements that the RAND researchers generated were based on a close analysis of the terrain and several other relevant factors. The findings suggest that to hold this territory the combat troop requirements to create a credible defense for external security and to manage internal security tasks could exceed 100,000, or one-third of the entire Russian Ground Forces, including conscripts.[76]

In a large-scale war, Russia's land forces could need to account for much more than a corner of northeastern Europe. The actions of other countries along Russia's border, such as Belarus and Ukraine, could require Russia to use its Ground Forces and VDV to maintain control of non-NATO countries (or regions within them) that it would not want to lose from its sphere of influence as a political outcome of the war. Were NATO to attempt to move ground forces into Ukraine or Belarus, this could lead to a situation after the war where NATO troops are permanently stationed from Esto-

---

[74] Richard Overy, *Russia's War: A History of the Soviet Effort: 1941–1945*, New York: Penguin, 1998, p. 60.

[75] Anthony Atler and Scott Boston, unpublished RAND Corporation research, 2020.

[76] In 2015, 48 percent of ground forces troops were conscripts. In 2016, the number of contract soldiers across the Russian armed forces increased by 30,000. From 2016 to 2020, there was little to no increase in contract soldiers. We therefore assume that the number of conscripts in the Ground Forces has not increased substantially since 2015. See Tebin, 2015, and Ministry of Defense of the Russian Federation, undated-c.

nia to Kyiv. This type of scenario, which we have not encountered in Russian military literature, assumes longer time frames than are often assumed by Russian officers publicly and would bring Russia's mobilization system into play. Russia's overall weakness vis-à-vis NATO also would likely dictate rapid offensive operations, both because Russia appears largely to reject attrition through defense as a concept and because the likely concern would not be a ground invasion of Russia but NATO occupation of territory that Russia considers to be within its sphere of influence.

It is not immediately clear how Russia imposes contact with NATO ground forces through offensive actions in the context of SOTMO. There is only a forming motor rifle division in Kaliningrad, while there are some 60,000 Polish land forces (three mechanized divisions and one armored cavalry division) and a rotational element of a U.S. armored brigade combat team and Army Aviation Task Force. Additional Russian ground forces could reinforce that formation, which would then need to move rapidly south and west to engage Polish and U.S. ground units (who themselves probably would be supported by NATO air power) unless the initial SAO was able to achieve some sort of air superiority. The ultimate political purpose of this movement could be to influence or replace the Polish government with one that would no longer be interested in NATO, which, in turn, would require a rather robust occupation of the country given popular sentiment toward Russia within Poland and a growing Polish territorial defense force that eventually could reach over 50,000 volunteers, although there have been some delays in recruitment.[77]

In Belarus, Russian ground operations would depend on the situation. If the political leadership sided with Russia and had control over the domestic situation in the country, the task of Russian forces would be to ensure the stability of the friendly regime and the territorial integrity of the country. The end result would be to take advantage of a destabilizing situation to create a slightly extended sphere of influence from the eastern Baltic Sea to Crimea.

The SOTMO of a scale described previously would create challenges for Russian ground forces as currently constructed. As mentioned, the ability of the SAO to reduce NATO air potential could give Russian ground for-

---

[77] "Poland to Build Territorial Defense Force by 2019," Deutsche Welle, November 14, 2016.

mations a freer hand to seize and hold territory. Russia's 150,000 Ground Forces personnel (perhaps 30 to 40 percent of whom are conscripts, depending on how conscripts are spread out across all of the military districts) in the Western and Southern Military Districts appear to be better suited for concentrated offensive action in one strategic direction in the initial period of war. But there are defense concerns across Russia's entire western border that would need to be managed in a large-scale war. Potential unrest—particularly in eastern Ukraine but also in Belarus, the countries of greatest importance to Russia—would likely require a significant portion of the ready Ground Forces formations in the respective OSKs.

Strategic Operation to Destroy Critically Important Targets

The most recent conceptual innovation within Russia's system of strategic actions is SODCIT. The character of warfare that emerged in practice in the early 1990s led Russian planners to consider a new form of employment of the armed forces. The ability to strike a target with conventional missiles with great precision over a distance of thousands of kilometers required updated operational concepts. At some point between 2004 and 2012, SODCIT (SOKVO or SOPVOP, in Russian) appeared in Russian military literature.

Little is known of the operation. The term SODCIT is not found in the MoD's Military-Encyclopedic Dictionary or other military dictionaries. A review of Russian military publications over the past three decades turned up only a few explicit references.[78] One of the earliest public discussions of SODCIT was in a 2009 presentation by Colonel O. Orlov, the Head of the Scientific Research Engineering Institute of the Russian Railway Troops. Orlov explained that the General Staff had prepared a new "system for the

---

[78] See A. A. Protasov, V. A. Sobolevskii, and V. V. Sukhorutchenko, "Planirovanie primeneniia strategicheskikh vooruzhenii," *Voennaia mysl'*, No. 7, 2014, p. 27; Ruchkin, 2012; and Goncharov, 2015.

forms of employing the Armed Forces to 2020."[79] These changes included the following actions:

> In peacetime, these are peacekeeping and special operations. In a period of heightened military threat—strategic deterrence and strategic deployment [of forces]. A feature of these forms is their implementation both in peacetime and in wartime. In wartime—strategic operations: a strategic operation to destroy critical enemy targets; a strategic aerospace operation; a strategic operation in the theater of military operations; [and a] strategic operation of the nuclear forces.[80]

In 2009, Russia was only beginning to build a strategic nonnuclear *triad*, which consisted of air-, sea-, and land-based systems and ISR to launch long-range PGM strikes across the European theater and U.S. territory. The kinetic components of the triad were much like those of Russian nuclear forces except with conventional payloads—the air-based Kh-101 Raduga, the air- and sea-based Kalibr, and the ground-based 9M728/9 missiles of the Iskander system. The required ISR infrastructure is being developed along with the missiles and delivery platforms to give the Russians the capability to employ conventional precision strike from ranges up to 4,000km.[81] As mentioned previously, Russia, as of early 2020, might have between 1,500 and 2,000 modern standoff missiles in its inventory. In essence, the long-range precision strike system fills a gap in the conflict escalation ladder and lengthens the bridge between conventional and nuclear war. Prior to the development of this capability, Russia felt that NATO possessed "escalation dominance" over it because of NATO's ability to conduct long-range, massed conventional strikes against forward targets or within Russia, while Russia would not have the ability to respond in kind with conventional weapons.

SODCIT appears to be a way to organize Russian planning with this nascent conventional long-range capability. The Russian military science

---

[79] A. Komarov, "Novaia tekhnika dlia novogo oblika zheleznodorozhnykh voisk," *Voennyi zheleznodorozhnik*, November 9, 2009.

[80] Komarov, 2009.

[81] Roger N. McDermott, "Tracing Russia's Path to Network-Centric Military Capability," blog post, Jamestown Foundation, December 4, 2020b.

community before and after the designation of the new strategic operation was weighing in on how to justify the force-to-damage requirements. This effort resembled the way in which Soviet military analysts thought about strategic nuclear weapons. In the case of strategic nuclear weapons, the discussion began with the question of how much damage was required such that the adversary would consider it unacceptable. Theoretically, this determination of unacceptability would lead to the numerical requirements of munitions, platforms, and associated military equipment. The ability to inflict unacceptable damage was at the heart of strategic nuclear deterrence.

Russian military experts essentially took the same approach in their analysis of long-range conventional munitions. Their adjustment has been to create a new concept known as *deterrence damage*. This has been defined in several ways; essentially, it refers to damage inflicted on *CITs*, which are most often defined as those related to critical military-industrial infrastructure—oil refineries, electric power stations, key enterprises—and hazardous sites, such as chemical factories and atomic energy stations.[82] In their work *Strategic Deterrence*, Burenok and Pechatnov proposed a novel methodology that incorporated elements of reflexive control, game theory, and expert surveys to develop deterrence damage criteria that would inform decisions on the composition and employment of strategic nonnuclear deterrence force groupings that would exist to serve as an additional layer of deterrence in peacetime and to conduct operations against critically important targets in wartime.[83] In the same work, which was published in 2011, the authors state that as long as the Russian inventory of long-range PGMs remained low, the most efficient and effective use of these limited assets was to use limited strikes against "countervalue" targets, such as power stations, oil refineries, or the facilities required to produce and deliver food and water

---

[82] A. A. Danilevich and O. P. Shunin, "O neiadernykh silakh sderzhivaniia," *Voennaia mysl*, No. 1, 1992. Russian focus on indirect or asymmetric approaches to warfare is not unlike the Air War Plans Division-1 of the late 1930s, which sought to rapidly destroy German air bases, electric power plants, transportation networks, oil refineries, aluminum plants, and other critical infrastructure without which planners assumed that it would be impossible to continue the war. See Malcolm Gladwell, *The Bomber Mafia*, Little, Brown and Company, New York, 2021, pp. 51–52.

[83] Burenok and Pechatnov, 2011, pp. 171–172.

to large urban areas to achieve psychological effects.[84] (A similar target list appeared approximately two decades earlier in an article by the long-time Soviet General Staff officer, A. A. Danilevich, and O. P. Shunin, and much of the article bears a striking resemblance to current Russian military discourse on the targeting of long-range conventional weapons.)[85] Employing nonstrategic nuclear weapons against hard military targets could compensate for the munitions shortfall until munitions numbers can be increased.[86]

In 2017, Gerasimov stated that, in the previous five years, Russia had made significant progress in the development of nonnuclear deterrence forces.[87] Gerasimov subsequently highlighted that "groupings of long-range cruise missile platforms—air, sea, and land—which are capable of deterrence in strategically important areas, have been created in each strategic direction."[88] In other words, in each military district, there are forces that are specifically designated to execute deterrence tasks—the destruction of critical military and nonmilitary infrastructure at long ranges (500–2,500km and up) with cruise and ballistic missiles to generate strategic effects. This tracks with what some Russian military analysts were proposing in 2011, which was that "a portion of the long-range precision munitions [should] be reserved by leadership to conduct special operations for the destruction of critically important targets."[89]

However, in the air domain, the only aircraft that are equipped to carry the Kh-101, a long-range air-launched cruise missile, are heavy bombers

---

[84] Burenok and Pechatnov, 2011, p. 150.

[85] Danilevich and Shunin, 1992, pp. 46–54.

[86] Burenok and Pechatnov, 2011, pp. 150–151.

[87] V. V. Gerasimov, "O khode vypolneniia ukazov prezidenta Rossiiskoi Federatsii ot 7 maia 2012 goda N603, 604 i razvitie vooruzhennykh sil Rossiiskoi Federatsii," *Voennaia mysl'*, No. 12, 2017, p. 8.

[88] V. V. Gerasimov, "Vliianie sovremennogo kharaktera vooruzhennoi bor'by na napravlennost' stroitel'stva i razvitiia Vooruzhennykh sil Rossiiskoi Federatsii. Prioritetnye zadachi voennoi nauki v obespechenii oborony strany," *Vestnik Akademii voennykh nauk*, Vol. 2, No. 63, 2018, p. 19.

[89] A. A. Protasov, V. A. Sobolevskii, V. V. Sukhorutchenko, and A. S. Borisenko, "Metodicheskoe obespechenie vyrabotki zamysla primeneniia VTO bol'shoi dal'nosti v operatsiiakh (boevikh deistviiakh)," *Voennaia mysl'*, No. 10, 2011, p. 40.

within Russia's Long Range Aviation Command, a component of the Strategic Nuclear Forces. It is possible that certain heavy bombers designated for conventional operations could be released to the OSK commander in wartime for this purpose. In the future, aircraft equipped with the air-launched ballistic missile Kinzhal likely will contribute to the targeting of military infrastructure during the SAO.[90] The remaining fighter aircraft, many of which are equipped with the Khibiny EW pods, will engage NATO air forces to the extent possible.

PGMs are part of Russia's strategic deterrence framework.[91] The coupling of long-range PGMs and deterrence, in our view, demonstrates that Russia is not thinking about these weapons exclusively as a conventional counterforce asset. Because *military deterrence* in Russia is defined as the ability to inflict damage on targets sufficient to have a significant psychological impact on the adversary, launching 60 cruise missiles at an air base or against SAM systems, for example, does not fit into Russia's strategic military deterrence construct. Therefore, it is likely that SODCIT is an operation using specially designated platforms to inflict deterrence damage against targets selected to generate maximum effect. According to a recent Russian article on modeling aviation strikes,

> The most important trend in the change in the character of armed combat is the prioritization of destroying the enemy's critically important targets (CIT), which leads to manmade disasters and the disruption of the enemy's military-economic potential. It is assumed that the maximum possible damage should be achieved as a result of strikes against CITs. Therefore, it is important to select for destruction those targets, strikes against which can lead to this result, including through a "cascade effect."[92]

---

[90] Discussions with one expert on Russian strategic weapons systems suggested that Kinzhal could be intended for use against NATO aircraft carriers depending on the capabilities of the terminal guidance of the missile. In early 2021, Russia announced that MiG-31BMs would be stationed in Novaia Zemlia in the far north as an experiment. See Russian Defense Policy, "Arctic Interceptors," blog post, January 18, 2021.

[91] President of Russia, *Voennaia doktrina Rossiiskoi Federatsii*, December 25, 2014.

[92] A. V. Ivantsov and A. V. Shalamov, "O modelirovanii protsessa mnogourovnevogo planirovaniia boevykh deistvii udarnoi aviatsii pri porazhenii kriticheskie vazhnykh

What Is a Critically Important Target?

A CIT is defined in Russian legislation as an "object whose loss of functionality would lead to the long-term loss of command and control, to the destruction of infrastructure, to the degradation or destruction of the economy of Russia . . . or to significant deterioration of the life of the Russian population."[93] The Russian Combined Arms Academy Training Center defines a CIT as "a key infrastructure facility or a grouping of troops (forces), the destruction (suppression) of which will lead to a guaranteed decrease in the enemy's combat capabilities and force him to abandon the achievement of the objectives of the operation being carried out (conduct of hostilities)."[94]

The categories and facilities listed in Table 4.3 are targets that Russia considers (within its own territory) critically important at the strategic-operational level. Chemical factories, oil refineries, hydroelectric dams, and atomic energy facilities are also among the most common targets mentioned in Russian literature and fit the general description of facilities whose destruction would lead to significant disruption of life or anthropogenic disasters.[95] Kokoshin's escalation ladder, shown in part of Figure 4.2, delineates between the phase of the war that involves targeting such objects as chemical factories and power stations and the phases that comprise more-traditional force-on-force warfighting. In keeping with other Russian thinking, the CIT destruction phase might be the bridge between conventional and nuclear war. In 2019, Burenok flatly stated, "The Americans understand

---

ob"ektov protivnika," *Voennaia mysl'*, No. 12, 2019, p. 92. Just prior to taking over his post as Commander of the VKS, General-Colonel Surovikin also wrote of the possibility of future operations seeking to create "manmade disasters." See Surovikin and Kuleshov, 2017, p. 8.

[93] President of Russia, "Osnovnye napraveleniia gosudarstvennoi politiki v oblasti obespecheniia bezopasnosti avtomatizirovannykh sistem upravleniia proizvodstvennymi i tekhnologicheskimi protsessami kriticheskie vazhnykh ob"etkov infrastruktury Rossiiskoi Federatsii," Order No. 803, February 3, 2012a.

[94] P. A. Dul'nev and V. I. Litvenenko, "Predlagaemye podkhody k obobshchennoi otsenke effektivnosti sredstv porazheniia, v tom chisle na novykh fizicheskikh printsipakh," *Vestnik Akademii voennykh nauk*, Vol. 2, No. 51, 2015, p. 150.

[95] See, for example, Kofman, Fink, and Edmonds, 2020, p. 54; and Timothy Thomas, *Kremlin Kontrol: Russia's Political-Military Reality*, Fort Leavenworth, Kan.: Foreign Military Studies Office, 2017, p. 128.

perfectly well that even in the case of an exclusively conventional war (which itself seems impossible) with Russia or China, the destruction of nuclear power plants, chemical plants, and dams is inevitable. After which civilized life (or life itself) on this territory will not be possible for many years or possibly forever."[96]

Much like employing nuclear weapons, this type of use of strategic non-nuclear weapons would be escalatory and unstable, to use Ogarkov's term. NATO would almost certainly have the ability to respond in kind with conventional munitions against similar targets on Russian territory. Moreover, counterforce strikes against traditional targets such as air bases, naval platforms, ports, logistics nodes, and key lines of communication historically have been planned for as part of SAO. These issues suggest that Russian planners may not consider SODCIT an opening gambit in the initial period of war but rather an act of survival where the benefits could conceivably outweigh the escalatory risks and military-economic costs. Relatedly, Russia may think of the capability to inflict deterrence damage against critical infrastructure primarily in the context of strategic deterrence as opposed to a viable military action in most circumstances. Burenok and Pechatnov themselves acknowledged the limitations of attacking critical economic targets with conventional weapons but stated that this course of action was imposed by capacity constraints.[97] At the same time, it is possible that some "key military facilities," as described by Burenok and Pechatnov, could be targeted early on, while the more sensitive economic targets could be reserved for a later phase of the conflict.[98] What is most important, is the idea that the Russians have developed an operational concept to potentially create catastrophic effects on NATO territory (or at least create the impression of a willingness to do so). NATO must therefore be prepared to defend against, mitigate (with civil defense), and counter Russian destruction of critical military-economic infrastructure, even in the initial period of a conflict.

---

[96] V. M. Burenok, "Kontseptual'nyi tupik," *Vooruzhenie i ekonomika*, Vol. 3, No. 49, 2019, p. 8. For a similar expression of this sentiment from nearly 20 years ago from another Russian expert on deterrence, see Tsygichko, 2002, p. 57.

[97] Burenok and Pechatnov, 2011, pp 151–152.

[98] Burenok and Pechatnov, 2011, p. 100; See also Kofman et al., 2021, p. 70.

Strategic Operation to Destroy Critically Important Targets, Nonstrategic Nuclear Weapons, and Other Possible Means

The limited evidence on SODCIT indicates that the Russians might see it as a final attempt to deescalate a large-scale war with NATO prior to employing nuclear weapons, which fall under the SONF. Russian discourse continually emphasizes the need to control escalation with the goal of containing a conflict at the lowest level possible.[99] However, based on what is known of Russia's PGM stockpile (as of 2019), a conventional SODCIT might not last very long, perhaps a few days. (Prospectively speaking, the new strategic weapon systems, such as the air-launched Kinzhal ballistic missile, could augment Russia's conventional stockpile.[100]) The nonnuclear deterrence (PGM) force groupings might be the primary formations for executing SODCIT, but until munitions numbers rise considerably, Russia will likely need to rely on nonstrategic nuclear weapons (NSNW) to inflict damage on NATO military and nonmilitary CITs after the conventional payloads have been exhausted.

Russian analysts have hinted that Russian NSNW are a way to compensate for the large PGM gap between the two sides.[101] Gerasimov spoke to this in remarks from 2017: "In the future, the acceleration of the production of high-precision weapons and the ongoing development of hypersonic missiles will make it possible to transfer the bulk of the strategic deterrence tasks from the nuclear to the nonnuclear sphere."[102] If Figure 4.1 is any guide, Russia is probably looking to the end of the 2020s or early 2030s to ensure a more credible nonnuclear deterrent option that, in wartime, could take the form of a fully conventional SODCIT of longer duration than a few days, depending on sortie rates. But production rates have reportedly not

---

[99] Kofman, Fink, and Edmonds, 2020.

[100] A. V. Evsiukov and A. L. Khriapin, "Rol' novykh sistem strategicheskikh vooruzhenii v obespechenii strategicheskogo sderzhivaniia," *Voennaia mysl'*, No. 12, 2020.

[101] Alexei Arbatov, Vladimir Dvorkin, and Sergey Oznobishchev, eds., *Russia and the Dilemmas of Nuclear Disarmament*, Moscow: Institute of World Economy and International Relations of the Russian Academy of Sciences, 2012, p. 114; Burenok and Pechatnov, 2011, p. 151.

[102] Gerasimov, 2017, p. 8.

been high. According to one source, Russia produced 300 Kalibr missiles from 2016 to 2019.[103]

Other emerging technology could augment current quantitative PGM shortfalls. Cyber tools and weapons, for example, have shown the ability to disrupt CITs, such as pipeline companies, industrial facilities, and electric power grids. It remains unclear how cyber weapons fit into Russian thinking on strategic operations and SODCIT in particular. But it would seem plausible that cyber weapons that are able to deliver similar effects as PGMs and NSNW could come to play a larger role in SODCIT. EW and anti–space laser systems are two other areas where the technology could become powerful and effective enough to generate the types of long-range effects that separate tactical weapons from the operational or strategic.

---

[103] S. F. Vikulov, ed., *Aktual'nye problemy realizatsii voenno-ekonomicheskogo potentsiala Rossii v pervoi chetverti XXI veka i osnovnye napravleniia voenno-ekonomicheskikh issledovanii*, Kniga 2, Kantsler, 2019, p. 101. See also, A. A. Dynkin, ed., *Mir 2035. Global'nyi prognoz*, Magistr, 2017, p. 261.

CHAPTER FIVE

Conclusion

Balance of Power

Despite justified Western emphases on the military challenges of Russia's local superiority, the Russian military takes a broader approach in its evaluation of weakness and strength. The MoD and the General Staff are assessing not only what is in place but what could be brought to bear in a crisis or over time. And this latent Western military capacity is undergirded by massive combined economies that produce some of the most-advanced technology in the world. As a result, Russian assessments and forecasts of military potential show a large power imbalance in favor of NATO for the next two decades. By itself, Russia would face considerable challenges in defeating NATO in a conventional war. Centuries of warfare have time and again shown that pursuit of decisive battle by the weaker side is most often an illusion that leads to protracted defeat for the overly optimistic aggressor.

Diplomacy with China

Although they are historical adversaries, Russia's embrace of improved relations with China is likely a tacit acknowledgement by Russia of the objective power dynamics of the present time. The Russo-Sino partnership contains numerous reasons to unravel, most prominently the increasingly stark asymmetry in the balance of power between the two countries. Not only does China possesses the largest standing military in the world, but annual Chinese military spending over the past decade has been three to four times more than Russia's.[1] Given China's growing military potential and its comparatively limitless reserves of manpower, if Russia were to build a force capable of challenging such an adversary, one can imagine the cost would be enormous.

Russia has instead taken a pragmatic, diplomatic approach, choosing cooperation over confrontation. One common goal seems to consistently unite the two: regime security. Beijing and Moscow share the view that the source of the threat arises from the West and its supposed fomenting of color revolutions with the objective of regime change.[2] They also share the view that the current international order—dominated by the U.S. and its allies, with liberal, democratic value given pride of place—is unacceptable.

Yet, the prospects of this partnership evolving into more than an alliance of convenience seem doubtful. Most recently, China took advantage of the collapse of global oil demand as a result of the COVID-19 pandemic to cheaply build a strategic oil reserves before curtailing its purchase of Middle Eastern oil in favor of Russian oil.[3] China thus maneuvered into a dominant position over Russia, cutting out other buyers and making Russia more dependent on China. This manipulation represents the exact behavior that observers argued could cause Moscow to reassess its partnership with China. Specifically, analysts have argued that such power plays could "generate resentment and a backlash in the Russian elite" at being relegated to the role of a "junior partner."[4] For now, though, Russian political elites have decreed that avoiding the cost of having to marshal large forces groupings along its western *and* eastern flanks is the preferable option.

Future War

With Russia's largest threat on its eastern flank to some extent pacified, future great power war is characterized by a high-intensity conflict in

---

[1] China Power, 2020.

[2] Kaczmarski, Katz, and Tiilikainen, 2018, p. 26.

[3] Kaczmarski, Katz, and Tiilikainen, 2018.

[4] Kaczmarski, Katz, and Tiilikainen, 2018, p. 59. See also Charap, Drennan, and Noël, 2017, p. 39.

the European theater. The scenario driving Russia's operational planning begins with widespread domestic unrest and evolves into a NATO conventional attack on Russian territory to undermine the regime and consolidate the position of the opposition. This forecast is based on NATO or Western actions in previous campaigns and the political outcomes of these conflicts. The war could evolve relatively quickly with little time to mobilize.

Russia sees NATO conventional long-range precision strikes on Russian territory as potentially decisive in the early phases of such a scenario. The war theoretically could be over in weeks or months, although this contradicts the idea that a military power with large material resources is not likely to be defeated quickly. Nevertheless, this is a crucial assumption that has influence on Russian development of force readiness and operational concepts. Most importantly, Russian officers have concluded that an orientation toward strategic defense and attrition in the initial period is not a viable strategy given the expected character of future war. This choice, if pursued genuinely, will likely increase requirements and costs, both in terms of readiness and conventional force structure.

Russian future war scenarios rest on another key assumption. Prior to attacking Russian territory, NATO has managed to build up a large invasion force. Previous studies put the number of U.S. fighters at well over 1,000, and involved multiple carrier strike groups, dozens of strategic bombers in the high north, hundreds of UAS, and cruise missile submarines in both the Arctic and Mediterranean regions. At the same time, these naval and maritime assets are highly mobile and at least theoretically could be moved into theater relatively quickly (though visibly in most cases). Because Russia is less focused on ground operations in future war, there is less public discussion of mobilization timelines for getting U.S. Army assets into Europe. It is the movement of air and naval assets that appears to be of foremost concern to Russian planners.

Trends in Force Readiness

Based on the aforementioned forecast of future war, Russia believes that having permanently ready forces is a key requirement. Professionalization and weapons modernization are the pillars of this effort, which centers on ready formations and combat units across the armed forces. These forces are likely what Russia would draw on in the initial period of war. In the land forces, the BTG is the ready maneuver element for a short-notice contingency without mobilization of any kind. Much less is known about permanently ready units elsewhere in the armed forces. This is a key gap, considering that Russia is most focused on NATO actions in the aerospace domain. Future studies will need to address this issue.

Russia's attention to its mobilization system since 2012–2013 complicates our analysis to some extent. If future war could occur quickly and be of short duration, the role of the state mobilization system is unclear. One possible explanation is that Russia is hedging against the possibility that future war could play out quite differently than in conflicts involving vastly mismatched adversaries. It could be longer, less dependent on technology, and more reliant on sheer mass. This outcome, however, is probably not advantageous for Russia because of overall resource disparities when compared with NATO, although China could play some augmenting role. Another explanation, which is not mutually exclusive of the first, is that Russia is worried about needing bodies to manage not just the NATO problem but also the internal security challenge if there were to be hundreds of thousands if not millions on the streets of Russian cities—a ubiquitous preoccupation of Russian political and military leaders.

Strategic Operations for Large-Scale War

Based on the previous discussion, the Russian General Staff has concluded that the only viable strategy to fight NATO is one based on preemption and destruction in the initial period. The expected character of future war shifts the emphasis toward Russia's SAO and SODCIT. SAO will pull on assets from across Russia to attempt to deny NATO air superiority, which could negate any Russian advantages on the ground.

Clearly, national air defenses are critical to defend Russian territory and possible forward forces (future war might not be as Russia imagines it). It is the offensive component that is most critical, however. Russia can shoot down NATO aircraft while itself suffering losses. But if Russia cannot limit sortie generation from air and sea and it cannot disrupt force flows from the

United States and within Europe, and it cannot degrade or destroy C4ISR linkages and assets, then the military potential calculation becomes much more consequential. Long-range ground-based fires also would be called on to fulfill these two tasks, but this is generally the purview of SAO, and possibly SODCIT.

SODCIT, based on the information we have reviewed to date, is more focused on attacking the underlying infrastructure and military-industrial potential of NATO countries in a future war. In short, SODCIT is the non-nuclear version of the strategic nuclear attack, and it might follow all other conventional attempts to inflict enough damage on NATO's ability to launch an aerospace attack within Russia. To be sure, there could be more-traditional military objectives of SODCIT that might change our view of sequence. But in that case, it would be difficult to differentiate from elements of SAO and SOTMO.

One wrinkle in Russian military discourse is that prioritization of targeting is evolving along with the character of warfare. Because the NATO aerospace attack is seen by Russia as the center of gravity of its operations, and because the attack is so dependent on the reliable transfer of digital information, the ability to successfully target NATO C4ISR enablers through kinetic and nonkinetic attack is arguably becoming the central objective of all Russian operational concepts in the initial period of war. We think this could be reflected in the trend discussed by Sterlin, Protasov, and Kreidin toward the eventual unification of strategic operations into a single operation that begins with conventionally targeting exclusively military assets, transitions to civilian infrastructure, and finally to nonstrategic and strategic nuclear weapons employment. The primary objective of this operation, in our view, would be to force NATO to either terminate the war or fight it in a way that is much less reliant on long-range precision strike. Russia wants to achieve these objectives overwhelmingly through preemption and destruction in the initial period of war. This preference is both because of and despite objective Russian weaknesses in military potential and because of a belief in the decisive nature of the conventional aerospace attack.

Abbreviations

ALCM	air-launched cruise missile
BTG	battalion tactical group
C2	command and control
C4ISR	command, control, communications, computers, intelligence, surveillance, and reconnaissance
CIT	critically important targets
COVID-19	coronavirus disease 2019
CSTO	Collective Security Treaty Organization
EW	electronic warfare
FSB	Federal Security Service
GDP	gross domestic product
HQ	headquarters
ISR	intelligence, surveillance, and reconnaissance
LRA	long-range aviation
MoD	Ministry of Defense
NATO	North Atlantic Treaty Organization
NSNW	nonstrategic nuclear weapons
OGPF	Operation of General-Purpose Forces
OSDF	Operation of the Strategic Deterrence Forces
OSK	Joint Strategic Command
PGM	precision-guided munition
PLA	People's Liberation Army
REB	electronic warfare (Russian)
SAM	surface-to-air missile
SAO	strategic aerospace operation

SCO	Shanghai Cooperation Organization
SLCM	submarine-launched cruise missile
SNF	strategic nuclear forces
SODCIT	strategic operation to destroy critically important targets
SONF	strategic operation of nuclear forces
SOTMO	strategic operation in the theater of military operations
TsSVI GSh	Center for Military-Strategic Research Under the General Staff
TVD	Theater of Military Operations
UAS	unmanned aerial system
UN	United Nations
USSR	Union of Soviet Socialist Republics
VDV	Airborne Troops
VKS	Aerospace Forces
VPO	military-political situation
VV MVD	Internal Troops of the Ministry of Internal Affairs

References

Adamsky, Dmitry (Dima), "If War Comes Tomorrow: Russian Thinking About 'Regional Nuclear Deterrence,'" *Journal of Slavic Military Studies*, Vol. 27, No. 1, 2014, pp. 163–188.

Adamsky, Dmitry (Dima), *Moscow's Aerospace Theory of Victory: Western Assumptions and Russian Reality*, Arlington, Va.: CNA, IOP-2021-U-029278-Final, February 2021.

Ageev, A. I., G. Mensch, and R. Matthews, eds., *Global Rating of Integral Power of 100 Countries 2012*, 3rd edition, Moscow: International Futures Research Academy, Institute for Economic Strategies, 2012.

Arbatov, Alexei, Vladimir Dvorkin, and Sergey Oznobishchev, eds., *Russia and the Dilemmas of Nuclear Disarmament*, Moscow: Institute of World Economy and International Relations of the Russian Academy of Sciences, 2012.

Baluevskii, Yurii, "Opiraias' na dostignutoe – idti dal'she i uverenee," *Rossiiskoe voennoe obozrenie*, No. 1, 2006, pp. 1–8.

Barndollar, Gil, "The Best or Worst of Both Worlds?" blog post, Center for Strategic and International Studies, September 23, 2020. As of July 12, 2021: https://www.csis.org/blogs/post-soviet-post/best-or-worst-both-worlds

Bartosh, A. A., "Strategicheskaia kul'tura kak instrument voenno-politicheskogo analiza," *Voennaia mysl'*, No. 7, 2020, pp. 7–8.

Bazhanov, Evgeniy, "Russian Perspectives on China's Foreign Policy and Military Development," in Jonathan D. Pollack and Richard H. Yang, eds., *In China's Shadow: Regional Perspectives on Chinese Foreign Policy and Military Development*, Santa Monica, Calif.: RAND Corporation, CF-137-CAPP, 1998, pp. 70–90. As of July 12, 2021: https://www.rand.org/pubs/conf_proceedings/CF137.html

Belokon', S. P., "Otsenivanie sostoianiia natsional'noi i voennoi bezopasnosti Rossii: ustanovlennyi poriadok i vozmozhnye puti sovershenstvovaniia," *Vestnik Moskovskogo gosudarstvennogo universiteta*, Seriia 25, *Mezhdunarodnye otnosheniia i mirovaia politika*, Vol. 1, 2018, pp. 20–41.

Bērziņš, Jānis, "The Theory and Practice of New Generation Warfare: The Case of Ukraine and Syria," *Journal of Slavic Military Studies*, Vol. 33, No. 3, 2020, pp. 355–380.

Blank, Stephen, "China's Military Base in Tajikistan: What Does it Mean?" blog post, Central Asia-Caucasus Analyst, April 18, 2019. As of January 8, 2021:
https://www.cacianalyst.org/publications/analytical-articles/item/13569-chinas-military-base-in-tajikistan-what-does-it-mean?.html

Borsin, V., and E. Bei, "Tema OGP dlia ofitserov '100-letie sozdaniia Krasnoi Armii,'" *Armeiskii sbornik*, No. 2, February 2018, pp. 49–56.

Boston, Scott, Michael Johnson, Nathan Beauchamp-Mustafaga, and Yvonne K. Crane, *Assessing the Conventional Force Imbalance in Europe: Implications for Countering Russian Local Superiority*, Santa Monica, Calif.: RAND Corporation, RR-2402, 2018. As of July 12, 2021:
https://www.rand.org/pubs/research_reports/RR2402.html

Buravlev, A. I., "K voprosu ob otsenke moguchchestva gosudarstva," *Vooruzhenie i ekonomika*, No. 1, 2016, pp. 20–32.

Burenok, V. M., "Razvitie systemy vooruzheniia i novyi oblik Vooruzhennykh sil RF," *Zashchita i bezopasnost'*, No. 2, 2009, pp. 14–16.

Burenok, V. M., "I grianet dron," *Voenno-promyshlennyi kur'er*, November 2, 2016.

Burenok, V. M., ed., *Kontseptiia obosnovaniia perspektivnogo oblika silovykh komponentov voennoi organizatsii Rossiiskoi Federatsii*, Moscow: Granitsa Publishing House, 2018a.

Burenok, Vasilii, "Oruzhie sudnogo dnia," *Zashchita i bezopasnost'*, Vol. 2, No. 85, 2018b, pp. 8–9.

Burenok, V. M., "Kontseptual'nyi tupik", *Vooruzhenie i ekonomika*, Vol. 3, No. 49, 2019, pp. 4–10.

Burenok, V. M., and Iu. A. Pechatnov, *Strategicheskoe sderzhivanie*, pre-publication copy, 2011, pp. 20–21.

Burutin, A. G., G. N. Vinokurov, V. M. Loborev, S. F. Pertsev, and Iu. A. Podkorytov, "Kotseptsiia nepriemlemogo ushcherba: genesis, osnovnye prichiny transformatsii, sovremennoe sostoianie," *Vooruzhenie. Politika. Konversiia*, No. 4, 2010, pp. 3–8.

Centre for Analysis of Strategies and Technologies, "Postavki boevykh samoletov v Voorzhennye Sily v 2019 godu," blog post, LiveJournal, January 16, 2020. As of September 30, 2021:
https://bmpd.livejournal.com/3907389.html

Charap, Samuel, John Drennan, and Pierre Noël, "Russia and China: A New Model of Great-Power Relations," *Survival*, Vol. 59, No. 1, February–March 2017, pp. 25–42.

Charap, Samuel, Dara Massicot, Miranda Priebe, Alyssa Demus, Clint Reach, Mark Stalczynski, Eugeniu Han, and Lynn E. Davis, *Russian Grand Strategy: Rhetoric and Reality*, Santa Monica, Calif.: RAND Corporation, RR-4238-A, 2021. As of October 1, 2021:
https://www.rand.org/pubs/research_reports/RR4238.html

Chekinov, S. G., and S. A. Bogdanov, "Evolutsiia sushchnosti i soderzhaniia poniatiia 'voina' v XXI stoletii," *Voennaia mysl'*, No. 1, 2017, pp. 30–43.

Chekinov, S. G., V. I. Makarov, and V. V. Kochergin, "Zavoevaniiu i uderzhaniiu gospodstva v vozdukhe (v vozdushno-kosmicheskoi sfere) - dostoinoe mesto v razvitii rossiiskoi voennoi teorii i podgotovke voisk (sil)," *Voennaia mysl'*, No. 2, 2017, pp. 58–66.

Chibisov, I. N., and V. A. Vodkin, "The Information-Strike Operation," *Armeiskii sbornik*, March 2011, pp. 46–49.

China Power, "What Does China Really Spend on Its Military?" webpage, Center for Strategic and International Studies, updated September 15, 2020. As of January 7, 2021:
https://chinapower.csis.org/military-spending/

"Chislennost' mobilizatsionnogo rezerva VS RF sostavit poriadka 9 tysiach," RIA Novosti, March 14, 2013.

Connable, Ben, Abby Doll, Alyssa Demus, Dara Massicot, Clint Reach, Anthony Atler, William Mackenzie, Matthew Povlock, and Lauren Skrabala, *Russia's Limit of Advance: Analysis of Russian Ground Force Deployment Capabilities and Limitations*, Santa Monica, Calif.: RAND Corporation, RR-2563-A, 2020. As of July 19, 2021:
https://www.rand.org/pubs/research_reports/RR2563.html

Connolly, Richard, and Mathieu Boulègue, *Russia's New State Armament Programme: Implications for the Russian Armed Forces and Military Capabilities to 2027*, London: Chatham House, Royal Institute of International Affairs, 2018.

Cooper, Julian, *The Russian State Armament Programme, 2018–2027*, Rome: NATO Defense College Research Division, Russian Studies, May 2018.

"Dal'niaia aviatsiia VKS RF. Dos'e," TASS, December 22, 2017.

Danilevich, A. A., and O. P. Shunin, "O neiadernykh silakh sderzhivaniia," *Voennaia mysl*, No. 1, 1992, pp. 48–53.

Dashkin, Iu. A., "Problemy moral'no-psikhologicheskogo obespecheniia i puti ikh resheniia," *Vestnik Akademii voennykh nauk*, Vol. 2, No. 27, 2009, pp. 39–42.

de Bloch, Jean, *The Future of War in Its Technical, Economic, and Political Relations*, trans. R. C. Long, Boston, Mass.: Ginn and Company, 1903.

"Defence Minister Rodionov Goes on the Warpath," *Izvestia*, December 27, 1996.

Demin, Andrei, "Ser'eznoi ugroze adekvatnyi otvet," *Voenno-promyshlennyi kur'er*, July 4, 2012.

Dick, Charles, *Russian Ground Forces: Posture Towards the West*, London: Chatham House, Royal Institute of International Affairs, April 2019.

"Doklad ministra oborony Rossiiskoi Federatsii na rasshirennom zasedanii kollegii Ministerstva oborony Rossiiskoi Federatsii 'Ob itogakh deiatel'nosti Ministerstva oborony Rossiiskoi Federatsii v 2008 godu s uchetom rezul'tatov finansovo-ekonomicheskoi raboty i zadachakh na 2009 god," *Na strazha Zapoliar'ia*, No. 23, March 21, 2009.

Dobbins, James, Howard J. Shatz, and Ali Wyne, *Russia Is a Rogue, Not a Peer; China Is a Peer, Not a Rogue: Different Challenges, Different Responses*, Santa Monica, Calif.: RAND Corporation, PE-310-A, 2019. As of July 14, 2021: https://www.rand.org/pubs/perspectives/PE310.html

Downs, Erica, "China-Russia Energy Relations: Why the Power of Siberia Pipeline Matters to China," blog post, CNA, December 18, 2019. As of December 23, 2020: https://www.cna.org/news/InDepth/article?ID=25

Dul'nev, P. A., and V. I. Litvenenko, "Predlagaemye podkhody k obobshchennoi otsenke effektivnosti sredstv porazheniia, v tom chisle na novykh fizicheskikh printsipakh," *Vestnik Akademii voennykh nauk*, Vol. 2, No. 51, 2015, pp. 147–151.

Dybov, V. N., and Yu. D. Podgornykh, "Aerospace Defense Stability in the Russian Federation," *Military Thought*, No. 4, 2019, pp. 24–32.

Dynkin, A. A., ed., *Mir 2035. Global'nyi prognoz*, Magistr, 2017, p. 261.

Eliseeva, Marina, "Uroki na vse vremena," *Krasnaia zvezda*, October 27, 2010.

Ellings, Richard J., and Robert Sutter, eds., *Axis of Authoritarians: Implications of China-Russia Cooperation*, Seattle, Wash.: National Bureau of Asian Research, 2018.

Erokhin, I. V., *Vozdushno-kosmicheskaia sfera i vooruzhennaia bor'ba*, Tver': Voennaia Akademiia Vozdushno-kosmichesakoi oborony, 2008.

"Evolutsiia kontrakta: 2007 god," *Rossiiskoe voennoe obozrenie*, No. 6, June 2007, pp. 50–52.

Evsiukov, A. V., and A. L. Khriapin, "Rol' novykh sistem strategicheskikh vooruzhenii v obespechenii strategicheskogo sderzhivaniia," *Voennaia mysl'*, No. 12, 2020, pp. 26–30.

Fedorov, Val'demar, and Aleksandr Tereshchenko, "Voennaia reforma: problemy i suzhdeniia. Armiia sil'na rezervom," *Krasnaia zvezda*, October 3, 1997.

Fedotov, I. A., "Napravleniia razvitiia operativno-strategicheskogo komandovaniia voennogo okruga na sovremennom etape stroitel'stva vooruzhennykh sil Rossiiskoi Federatsii," *Vestnik Akademii voennykh nauk*, Vol. 4, No. 57, 2016, pp. 65–69.

Fenenko, A. V., "Faktor takticheskogo iadernogo oruzhiia v mirovoi politike," *Vestnik Moskovskogo universiteta*, Seriia 25, *Mezhdunarodnaia otnosheniia i mirovaia politika*, No. 2, 2012. As of February 22, 2021: https://cyberleninka.ru/article/n/ faktor-takticheskogo-yadernogo-oruzhiya-v-mirovoy-politike

FitzGerald, Mary, *Changing Soviet Doctrine on Nuclear War*, Alexandria, Va.: CNA, October 1986a.

FitzGerald, Mary, "Marshal Ogarkov on the Modern Theater Operation," *Naval War College Review*, Vol. 39, No. 4, Autumn 1986b, pp. 6–25.

FitzGerald, Mary C., "The Russian Military's Strategy for 'Sixth Generation' Warfare," *Orbis*, Vol. 38, No. 3, Summer 1994, pp. 457–476.

FitzGerald, Mary C., "China's Evolving Military Juggernaut," in *China's New Great Leap Forward: High Technology and Military Power in the Next Half-Century*, Washington, D.C.: Hudson Institute, 2005, pp. 35–86.

Freedman, Lawrence, *The Future of War: A History*, New York: PublicAffairs, 2017.

"FTsP: Podvedenie itogov," *Krasnaia zvezda*, October 20, 2007.

Gady, Franz-Stefan, "China, Russia Conduct First Joint Live-Fire Missile Exercise at Sea," blog post, *The Diplomat*, May 8, 2019. As of January 7, 2021: https://thediplomat.com/2019/05/ china-russia-conduct-first-joint-live-fire-missile-exercise-at-sea/

Galenovich, Yuri M., *The Mandates of Jiang Zemin*, Moscow: Muravey, 2003.

Gareev, Makhmut, "Ob organizatsii voennogo upravleniia na strategicheskikh napravleniiakh," *Natsional'naia oborona*, No. 10, October 2010.

Gareev, M. A., "Problemy sovremennoi sistemy voennogo upravleniia i puti ee sovershenstvovaniia s uchetom novykh oboronnykh zadach i izmenenii kharaktera budushchikh voin," *Voennaia mysl'*, No. 5, 2004, pp. 66–79.

Gilli, Andrea, and Mauro Gilli, "Why China Has Not Caught Up Yet: Military-Technological Superiority and the Limits of Imitation, Reverse Engineering, and Cyber Espionage," *International Security*, Vol. 43, No. 3, Winter 2018/19, pp. 141–189.

Glantz, David M., *The Military Strategy of the Soviet Union: A History*, Frank Cass and Co., 1992.

Gerasimov, V. V., "Rol' General'nogo shtabe v organizatsii oborony strany v sootvetstvii s novym polozheniem o General'nom shtabe, utverzhdennym prezidenta Rossiiskoi Federatsii," *Vestnik Akademii voennykh nauk*, Vol. 1, No. 46, 2014, p. 16.

Gerasimov, V. V., "Opyt strategicheskogo rukovodstva v velikoi otechestvennoi voiny i organizatsiia edinogo upravleniia oboronoi strany v sovremennykh usloviiakh," *Vestnik Akademii voennykh nauk*, Vol. 2, No. 51, 2015, pp. 5–15.

Gerasimov, V. V., "O khode vypolneniia ukazov prezidenta Rossiiskoi Federatsii ot 7 maia 2012 goda N603, 604 i razvitie vooruzhennykh sil Rossiiskoi Federatsii," *Voennaia mysl'*, No. 12, 2017, pp. 7–21.

Gerasimov, V. V., "Vliianie sovremennogo kharaktera vooruzhennoi bor'by na napravlennost' stroitel'stva i razvitiia Vooruzhennykh sil Rossiiskoi Federatsii. Prioritetnye zadachi voennoi nauki v obespecheniia oborony strany," *Vestnik Akademii voennykh nauk*, Vol. 2, No. 63, 2018, pp. 16–22.

Gerasimov, V. V., "Razvitie voennoi strategii v sovremennykh usloviiakh. Zadachi voennoi nauki," *Vestnik Akademii voennykh nauk*, Vol. 2, No. 67, 2019, pp. 6–11.

Gladwell, Malcolm, *The Bomber Mafia*, Little, Brown and Company, New York, 2021, pp. 51–52.

Goncharov, Andrei, "Voina budet vo vsekh sredakh," *Vozdushno-kosmicheskaia sfera*, No. 6, 2015, pp. 51–57.

Gosudarstvennaia Duma, "Vladimir Shamanov: Priniat zakon po dopolnitel'nym meram sotsial'noi podderzhki voennosluzhashchikh," webpage, December 18, 2018. As of July 13, 2021:
http://duma.gov.ru/news/29266/

Government of Russia, "O federal'noi tselevoi programme 'Perekhod k komplektovaniiu voennosluzhashchimi, prokhodiashchimi voennuiu sluzhbu po kontraktu, riada soedinenii i voinskikh chastei' na 2004–2007 gody," No. 523, August 25, 2003.

Government of Russia, "O statuse voennosluzhashchikh," Federal Law No. 76-FZ, December 8, 2020.

Grisé, Michelle, Alyssa A. Demus, Yuliya Shokh, Marta Kepe, Jonathan Welburn, and Khrystyna Holynska, *Rivalry in the Information Sphere: Russian Conceptions of Information Confrontation*, Santa Monica, Calif.: RAND Corporation, RR-A198-8, 2022. As of August 18, 2022:
https://www.rand.org/pubs/research_reports/RRA198-8.html

Grudinin, I. V., D. G. Maiburov, and V. V. Klimov, "Strukturno-funktsional'nyi analiz protsessa otrazheniia udara stredstv vozdushno-kosmicheskogo napadeniia protivnika," *Vestnik Akademii voennykh nauk*, Vol. 3, No. 72, 2020, pp. 71–80.

Hagström Frisell, Eva, and Krister Pallin, eds., *Western Military Capability in Northern Europe 2020*, Part I: *Collective Defence*, Stockholm: Swedish Defence Research Agency, FOI-R--5012--SE, February 2021.

Hoehn, John R., "Defense Primer: U.S. Precision-Guided Munitions," Washington, D.C.: Congressional Research Service, IF11353, updated June 4, 2021.

Hoffenaar, Jan, and Christopher Findlay, eds., *Military Planning for European Theatre Conflict During the Cold War: An Oral History Roundtable*, Zurich: Center for Security Studies ETH Zurich, 2007.

Hsu, Immanuel C. Y., *The Rise of Modern China*, New York: Oxford University Press, 1970.

Iagol'nikov, S. V., "Voenno-tekhnicheskie aspekty organizatsii i vedeniia vozdushno-kosmicheskoi oborony v sovremennykh usloviiakh," *Vestnik Akademii voennykh nauk*, Vol. 2, No. 59, 2017, pp. 61–62.

Iagol'nikov, S. V., "Organizatsiia vozdushno-kosmicheskoi oborony v sovremennykh usloviiakh," *Vestnik Akademii voennykh nauk,* Vol. 2, No. 55, 2016, pp. 47–50.

International Institute for Strategic Studies, *Military Balance*, Vol. 120, London: Routledge, 2020.

International Institute for Strategic Studies, *Military Balance*, Vol. 121, London: Routledge, 2021.

Ivanov, V. G., A. Iu. Savitskii, and S. G. Makarov, "Bliianie voin i vooruzhennykh konfliktov na sistemu sviazi voennogo naznacheniia," in *Radiolokatsiia, navigatsiia, sviaz': Sbornik trudov XXVI Mezhdunarodnoi nauchno-tekhnicheskoi konferentsii*, Tom 2, Voronezhskii gosudarstvennoi universitet / Sozvezdie Contsern, 2020.

Ivanov, Sergei, "The Priority Tasks of the Development of the Armed Forces of the Russian Federation," Ministry of Defense of the Russian Federation, 2003.

Ivantsov, A. V., and A. V. Shalamov, "O modelirovanii protsessa mnogourovnevogo planirovaniia boevykh deistvii udarnoi aviatsii pri porazheniia kriticheskie vazhnykh ob"ektov protivnika," *Voennaia mysl'*, No. 12, 2019, pp. 92–98.

Johnson, Dave, "VOSTOK 2018: Ten Years of Russian Strategic Exercises and Warfare Preparation," webpage, *NATO Review*, December 20, 2018.

Kaczmarski, Marcin, Mark N. Katz, and Teija Tiilikainen, *The Sino-Russian and US-Russian Relationships: Current Developments and Future Trends*, No. 57, Helsinki: Finish Institute of International Affairs, December 2018.

Kartapolov, Andrei, "Uroki voennykh konfliktov, perspektivy razvitiia sredstv i sposobov ikh vedeniia. Priamye i nepriamye deistviya v sovremennykh mezhdunarodnyh konfliktakh," *Vestnik Akademii voennykh nauk*, Vol. 2, No. 51, 2015, pp. 26–36.

Kashcheev, A. M., Iu. A. Malinovskii, and A. M. Sazonov, "Regional'nye tsentry upravleniia sub"ektov Rossiiskoi Federatsii v sistema upravleniia territorial'noi oboronoi," *Vestnik Akademii voennykh nauk*, Vol. 1, No. 70, 2020, pp. 76–77.

Kashin, Vasily, "Russia and China Take Military Partnership to New Level," *Moscow Times*, October 23, 2019.

"KB 'Iuzhnoe' izgotovilo opytnyi ekzemliar OTRK 'Grom-2' ['Iuzhnoe' Design Bureau Builds Prototype Example of 'Grom-2' Missile System]," *Novosti VPK*, April 23, 2019. As of February 22, 2021: https://vpk.name/news/274678_kb_yuzhnoe_izgotovilo_opyitnyii_ ekzemplyar_otrk_grom2.html

Khramchikhin, Alexander, "Prezhdevremennyi otkaz ot broni," *Nezavisamoye voennoye obozreniye*, February 20, 2020.

Khramchikhin, Anatolii, "Voiska mirnogo neba," *Nezavisimoe voennoe obozrenie*, November 22, 2018.

Khodarenok, Mikhail, "Ot chego zavisit pobeda," *Vozdushno-kosmicheskaia sfera*, No. 5, 2004, pp. 4–8.

Khodarenok, Mikhail, "Voennye reform ispytyvaiut defitsit novatorstva. Organizatsionno-shtatnye meropriiatiia v Vooruzhennykh silakh dvizhutsia po zamknutomu krugu," *Nezavisimoe voennoe obozrenie*, July 20, 2001.

Khomutov, A. V., "O reshenii problem primeneniia obshchevoiskovykh formirovanii takticheskogo zvena v sovremennykh voennykh konfliktakh," *Voennaia mysl'*, No. 6, 2020, pp. 56–57.

Kipp, Jacob, "General-Major A. A. Svechin and Modern Warfare: Military History and Military Theory," in Aleksandr A. Svechin, *Strategy*, Kent D. Lee, ed., Minneapolis, Minn.: East View Publications, 1992, pp. 23–60.

Kipp, Jacob W., "A Review of: 'Vladimir Slipchenko and Makhmut Gareev,'" *Journal of Slavic Military Studies*, Vol. 20, No. 1, 2007a, pp. 147–158.

Kipp, Jacob, "Introduction," in Makhmut Gareev and Vladimir Slipchenko, *Future War*, trans., Fort Leavenworth, Kan.: Foreign Military Studies Office, 2007b.

Kjellén, Jonas, *Russian Electronic Warfare: The Role of Electronic Warfare in the Russian Armed Forces*, Stockholm: Swedish Defense Research Agency, FOI-R--4625--SE, 2018.

Klimenko, A. F., and V. I. Lutovinov, "We May Endanger Russia's Military Security by Misrepresenting Real Threats," *Military Thought*, No. 4, 2001, pp. 69–72.

Kofman, Michael, "Russian A2/AD: It Is Not Overrated, Just Poorly Understood," blog post, Russian Military Analysis, January 25, 2020. As of December 9, 2020:
https://russianmilitaryanalysis.wordpress.com/2020/01/25/russian-a2-ad-it-is-not-overrated-just-poorly-understood/

Kofman, Michael, Anya Fink, and Jeffrey Edmonds, *Russian Strategy for Escalation Management: Evolution of Key Concepts*," Arlington, Va.: CNA, DRM-2019-U-022455-1Rev, April 2020.

Kokoshin, A. A., *Vydaiushchiisia voennyi teoretik i voenachal'nik Aleksandr Andreevich Svechin. O ego zhizni, ideiakh, trudakh i nasledii dlia nastoiashchego i budushchego*, Moscow: Izdatel'stvo Moskovskogo universiteta, 2013.

Kokoshin, Andrei, "Neskol'ko izmerenii voiny," *Voprosy filosofii*, No. 8, 2016, pp. 15–16.

Kokoshin, A. A., *Voprosy prikladnoi teorii voiny*, Moscow: Izdatel'skii dom Vysshei shkoly ekonomiki, 2018.

Kokoshin, A. A., and V. V. Larionov, "Origins of the Intellectual Rehabilitation of A. A. Svechin," in Aleksandr A. Svechin, *Strategy*, Kent D. Lee, ed., Minneapolis, Minn.: East View Publications, 1991, pp. 1–14.

Kollektsioner Baionov, "Postavki sistem protivovozdushnoi oborony v Vooruzhennye Sily Rossii v 2020 g." blog post, LiveJournal, January 9, 2021. As of September 14, 2021:
https://altyn73.livejournal.com/2021/01/09/

Komarov, A., "Novaia tekhnika dlia novogo oblika zheleznodorozhnykh voisk," *Voennyi zheleznodorozhnik*, November 9, 2009.

Konstantinov, V., and A. Stepanov, "Razvitie teorii i praktika boevogo primeneniia raketnykh voisk i artillerii v armeiskikh operatsiakh," *Zashchita i bezopasnost'*, No. 3, 2009, pp. 30–33.

KonsultantPlus, "Obzor izmenenii Federalnogo zakona ot 27.05.1998 N 76-FZ 'O statuse voennosluzhashchikh'," webpage, December 27, 2018. As of July 19, 2021:
https://www.consultant.ru/document/cons_doc_LAW_76682/ef830b5062e74c308b854f636257f40a07e98fca/

Korchak, V. Iu., R. V. Reulov, S. V. Stukalin, and S. A. Grigor'eva, "Nauchno-metodicheskie osnovy voenno-tekhnicheskoi otsenki nauchnykh i tekhnologicheskikh dostizhenii organizatsii Rossiiskoi Akademii nauk, vysshei shkoly i predpriiatii promyshlennosti," *Vestnik Akademii voennykh nauk*, Vol. 2, No. 55, 2016, pp. 145–151.

Kovalev, V. I., "Iadernoe bezopasnosti Rossii v XXI veke," *Strategicheskaia stabil'nost'*, Vol. 3, No. 68, 2014, pp. 16–17.

Kozak, Iulia, "Pravo stat' zashchitnikom rodiny," *Krasnaia zvezda*, October 2, 2017.

Kozak, Iulia, "Prizyv vo imia bezopasnosti otechestva," *Krasnaia zvezda*, October 24, 2018.

Kravchenko, Viktor, "Flot v sovremennoi voine," *Morskaia gazeta*, April 17, 2003.

Lazukin, V. F., I. I. Korolyov, and V. N. Pavlov, "On Basic Elements of Electronic Warfare Forces Tactics," *Military Thought*, Vol. 26, No. 4, 2017, pp. 29–35.

Li, Dan Ting, Dararat Mattariganond, and Benjawan Narasaj, "The Opium Wars in China's Junior High School Textbooks," *Journal of Mekong Societies*, Vol. 15, No. 2, May–August 2019, pp. 86–101.

Makarov, N. E., "Tezisy vystupleniia nachal'nika General'nogo shtabe Vooruzhennykh Sil Rossiiskoi Federatsii – pervogo zamestitelia Ministra oborony Rossiiskoi Federatsii generala armii N. E. Makarova," *Vestnik Akademii voennykh nauk*, Vol. 1, No. 26, 2009a, pp. 19–23.

Makarov, Nikolai, "Armiia XXI veka," *Voenno-promyshlennyi kur'er*, June 17, 2009b.

Markov, S. V., "O nekotoryk podkhodakh k opredeleniyu sushchnosti informatsionnogo oruzhiya [Several Approaches to the Determination of the Essence of the Information Weapon]," *Bezopasnost [Security]*, Nos. 1–2, 1996, pp. 45–59.

Maskin, V. M., "K voprosu o soderzhanii soedinenii i voinskikh chastei v kategorii postoiannoi gotovnosti," *Voennaia mysl'*, No. 1, 2010, pp. 26–30.

McDermott, Roger N., "Zapad 2009 Rehearses Countering a NATO Attack on Belarus," *Eurasia Daily Monitor*, Vol. 6, No. 179, September 30, 2009.

McDermott, Roger N., "Russian Military Prepares for Vostok 2010," *Eurasia Daily Monitor*, Vol. 7, No. 106, June 2, 2010.

McDermott, Roger N., *Russian Perspective on Network-Centric Warfare: The Key Aim of Serdyukov's Reform*, Fort Leavenworth, Kan.: Foreign Military Studies Office, 2011.

McDermott, Roger N., "Russia's Impact on Nuclear Policy in China: Cooperative Trends and Depth of Influence," *Journal of Slavic Military Studies*, Vol. 33, No. 1, 2020a, pp. 44–88.

McDermott, Roger N., "Tracing Russia's Path to Network-Centric Military Capability," blog post, Jamestown Foundation, December 4, 2020b. As of July 13, 2021:
https://jamestown.org/program/
tracing-russias-path-to-network-centric-military-capability/

Mearsheimer, John J., *The Tragedy of Great Power Politics*, New York: W. W. Norton and Company, 2001.

Mikhailova, Diana, "Osobennosti novykh divizii sukhoputnykh voisk Rossii. Chast' 1," blog post, November 7, 2018. As of September 30, 2021:
https://diana-mihailova.livejournal.com/2919361.html

Mikhalev, S. N., *Voennaia strategiia. Podgotovka i vedenie voin novogo i noveishego vremeni*, Kuchkovo pole, 2003.

Ministry of Defense of the Russian Federation, "Strategicheskaia operatsiia iadernykh sil (SOYAS)," webpage, *Russian Military Encyclopedia*, undated-a. As of July 13, 2021:
https://encyclopedia.mil.ru/encyclopedia/dictionary/details.htm?id=14375@
morfDictionary

Ministry of Defense of the Russian Federation, "Strategicheskaia vozdushno-kosmicheskaia operatsiia," webpage, *Russian Military Encyclopedia*, undated-b. As of January 28, 2021:
https://encyclopedia.mil.ru/encyclopedia/dictionary/details.htm?id=10372@
morfDictionary

Ministry of Defense of the Russian Federation, "Strategicheskie yaderniye sili," presentation, undated-c. As of February 4, 2021:
http://mil.ru/files/files/2012-2020.pdf

Ministry of Defense of the Russian Federation, "Vystuplenie Ministra oborony Rossiiskoi Federatsii generala armii Sergeia Shoigu na rasshirennom zasedanii Kollegii Minoborony Rossii," December 22, 2016.

Moiseev, M. A., "Strategicheskie zadeli Marshala Ogarkova," *Krasnaia zvezda*, October 26, 2007.

Mueller, Karl P., ed., *Precision and Purpose: Airpower in the Libyan Civil War*, Santa Monica, Calif.: RAND Corporation, RR-676-AF, 2015. As of July 13, 2021:
https://www.rand.org/pubs/research_reports/RR676.html

Nolan, Cathal J., *The Allure of Battle: A History of How Wars Have Been Won and Lost*, New York: Oxford University Press, 2017.

Ochmanek, David, Peter A. Wilson, Brenna Allen, John Speed Meyers, and Carter C. Price, *U.S. Military Capabilities and Forces for a Dangerous World*, Santa Monica, Calif.: RAND Corporation, RR-1782-1-RC, 2017. As of July 14, 2021:
https://www.rand.org/pubs/research_reports/RR1782-1.html

Office of the Secretary of Defense, *Military and Security Developments Involving the People's Republic of China 2020: Annual Report to Congress*, Washington, D.C.: U.S. Department of Defense, 2020.

"Ofitsial'nyi otdel," *Morskoi sbornik*, No. 1, January 2013, pp. 11–43.

Osnos, Evan, David Remnick, and Joshua Yaffa, "Trump, Putin, and the New Cold War," *New Yorker*, February 24, 2017.

Osokina, Elena, *Za fasadom "sotsialisticheskogo izobiliia": Raspredelenie i rynok v snabzhenii naseleniia v gody industrializatsii, 1927–1941*, 2nd ed., Moscow, 2008.

Ostankov, Vladimir, "Voiny budushchego nachinaiutsia segodnia," *Voenno-promyshlennyi kur'er*, October 15, 2019.

Ostankov, V. I., "Strategicheskikh rezervov net," *Voenno-promyshlennyi kur'er*, March 17, 2014.

Overy, Richard, *Russia's War: A History of the Soviet Effort: 1941–1945*, New York: Penguin, 1998.

Pechatnov, Iu. A., "Metodicheskii podkhod k opredeleniiu sderzhivaiushchego ushcherba s uchetom sub"ektivnykh osobennostei ego vospriiatiia veroiatnym protivnikom," *Vooruzheniia i ekonomika*, Vol. 3, 2011, pp. 23–30.

Perović, Jeronim, and Benno Zogg, "Russia and China: The Potential of Their Partnership," *CSS Analyses in Security Policy*, Center for Security Studies, ETH Zurich, No. 250, October 2019.

"Poland to Build Territorial Defense Force by 2019," Deutsche Welle, November 14, 2016.

Popov, I. M., and M. M. Khamzatov, *Voina budushchego: kontseptsual'nye osnovy i prakticheskie vyvody*, Moscow: Kuchkovo pole, 2018.

Posen, Barry R., "Europe Can Defend Itself," *Survival*, Vol. 62, No. 6, December 2020–January 2021, pp. 7–34.

President of Russia, "Osnovnye napraveleniia gosudarstvennoi politiki v oblasti obespecheniia bezopasnosti avtomatizirovannykh sistem upravleniia proizvodstvennymi i tekhnologicheskimi protsessami kriticheskie vazhnykh ob"etkov infrastruktury Rossiiskoi Federatsii," Order No. 803, February 3, 2012a.

President of Russia, "O vnesenii izmenenii v otdel'nye zakonodatel'nye akty Rossiiskoi Federatsii po voprosam sozdaniia mobilizatsionnogo liudskogo rezerva," Federal Law No. 288-FZ, December 30, 2012b.

President of Russia, "Ob oborone," Federal Law No. 61-FZ, December 30, 2012c.

President of Russia, "O vnesenii izmenenii v otdel'nye zakonodatel'nye akty Rossiiskoi Federatsii," Federal Law No. 55-FZ, April 5, 2013.

President of Russia, *Voennaia doktrina Rossiiskoi Federatsii*, December 25, 2014.

President of Russia, "O sozdanii mobilizatsionnogo liudskogo rezerva Vooruzhennykh Sil Rossiiskoi Federatsii," Order No. 370, July 17, 2015.

President of Russia, "O prizyve v aprele – iiule 2016 g. grazhdan Rossiiskoi Federatsii na voennuiu sluzhbu i ob uvol'nenii s voennoi sluzhby grazhdan, prokhodiashchikh voennuiu sluzhbu po prizyvu," Order No. 139, March 31, 2016a.

President of Russia, "O prizyve v oktiabre – dekabre 2016 g. grazhdan Rossiiskoi Federatsii na voennuiu sluzhbu i ob uvol'nenii s voennoi sluzhby grazhdan, prokhodiashchikh voennuiu sluzhbu po prizyvu," Order No. 503, October 3, 2016b.

President of Russia, "O prizyve v aprele – iiule 2017 g. grazhdan Rossiiskoi Federatsii na voennuiu sluzhbu i ob uvol'nenii s voennoi sluzhby grazhdan, prokhodiashchikh voennuiu sluzhbu po prizyvu," Order No. 135, March 31, 2017a.

President of Russia, "O prizyve v oktiabre – dekabre 2017 g. grazhdan Rossiiskoi Federatsii na voennuiu sluzhbu i ob uvol'nenii s voennoi sluzhby grazhdan, prokhodiashchikh voennuiu sluzhbu po prizyvu," Order No. 445, September 29, 2017b.

President of Russia, "Ob ustanovlenii shtatnoi chislennosti Vooruzhennykh sil Rossiiskoi Federatsii, Order No. 555, November 17, 2017c.

President of Russia, "O prizyve v aprele – iiule 2018 g. grazhdan Rossiiskoi Federatsii na voennuiu sluzhbu i ob uvol'nenii s voennoi sluzhby grazhdan, prokhodiashchikh voennuiu sluzhbu po prizyvu," Order No. 129, April 2, 2018a.

President of Russia, "O prizyve v oktiabre – dekabre 2018 g. grazhdan Rossiiskoi Federatsii na voennuiu sluzhbu i ob uvol'nenii s voennoi sluzhby grazhdan, prokhodiashchikh voennuiu sluzhbu po prizyvu," Order No. 552, September 28, 2018b.

President of Russia, "O prizyve v aprele – iiule 2019 g. grazhdan Rossiiskoi Federatsii na voennuiu sluzhbu i ob uvol'nenii s voennoi sluzhby grazhdan, prokhodiashchikh voennuiu sluzhbu po prizyvu," Order No. 135, April 1, 2019a.

President of Russia, "O prizyve v oktiabre – dekabre 2019 g. grazhdan Rossiiskoi Federatsii na voennuiu sluzhbu i ob uvol'nenii s voennoi sluzhby grazhdan, prokhodiashchikh voennuiu sluzhbu po prizyvu," Order No. 472, October 2, 2019b.

President of Russia, "O prizyve v aprele – iiule 2020 g. grazhdan Rossiiskoi Federatsii na voennuiu sluzhbu i ob uvol'nenii s voennoi sluzhby grazhdan, prokhodiashchikh voennuiu sluzhbu po prizyvu," Order No. 232, March 30, 2020a.

President of Russia, *Basic Principles of State Policy of the Russian Federation on Nuclear Deterrence*, Moscow: Ministry of Foreign Affairs of the Russian Federation, June 8, 2020b.

President of Russia, "O prizyve v oktiabre – dekabre 2020 g. grazhdan Rossiiskoi Federatsii na voennuiu sluzhbu i ob uvol'nenii s voennoi sluzhby grazhdan, prokhodiashchikh voennuiu sluzhbu po prizyvu," Order No. 581, October 1, 2020c.

President of Russia, "O statuse voennosluzhashchikh," Federal Law No. 76-FZ, December 8, 2020d.

Protasov, A. A., V. A. Sobolevskii, and V. V. Sukhorutchenko, "Planirovanie primeneniia strategicheskikh vooruzhenii," *Voennaia mysl'*, No. 7, 2014, pp. 9–27.

Protasov, A. A., V. A. Sobolevskii, V. V. Sukhorutchenko, and A. S. Borisenko, "Metodicheskoe obespechenie vyrabotki zamysla primeneniia VTO bol'shoi dal'nosti v operatsiiakh (boevikh deistviiakh)," *Voennaia mysl'*, No. 10, 2011, pp. 36–48.

"Putin: China Is Strategic Partner," *UPI*, Moscow, July 16, 2000.

"Putin zaiavil o postepennom ukhode ot sluzhby po prizyvu," *Izvestiya*, October 24, 2017.

Radin, Andrew, Lynn E. Davis, Edward Geist, Eugeniu Han, Dara Massicot, Matthew Povlock, Clint Reach, Scott Boston, Samuel Charap, William Mackenzie, Katya Migacheva, Trevor Johnston, and Austin Long, *The Future of the Russian Military: Russia's Ground Combat Capabilities and Implications for U.S.-Russia Competition*, Santa Monica, Calif.: RAND Corporation, RR-3099-A, 2019. As of July 13, 2021: https://www.rand.org/pubs/research_reports/RR3099.html

Reach, Clint, Alyssa Demus, Eugenieu Han, Bilyana Lilly, Krystyna Marcinek, and Yuliya Shokh, *Russian Military Forecasting and Analysis: The Military-Political Situation and Military Potential in Strategic Planning*, Santa Monica, Calif.: RAND Corporation, RR-A198-4, 2022. As of August 18, 2022:
https://www.rand.org/pubs/research_reports/RRA198-4.html

Reach, Clint, Vikram Kalambi, and Mark Cozad, *Russian Assessments and Applications of the Correlation of Forces and Means*, Santa Monica, Calif.: RAND Corporation, RR-4235-OSD, 2020. As of July 13, 2021:
https://www.rand.org/pubs/research_reports/RR4235.html

Rogozin, D. O., ed., *Voina i mir v terminakh i opredeleniiakh*, Moscow: Veche, 2017.

Rostovskii, Mikhail, "Sergei Shoigu rasskazal, kak spasali rossiiskuiu armiiu," *Moskovskii komsomolets*, September 22, 2019.

Ruchkin, S. V., *Podkhod k vyboru pokazatelei effektivnosti porazheniia ob"ektov protivnika iadernym oruzhiem i strategicheskim neiadernym oruzhiem*, XXXI Vserossiiskaia NTK, Chast' 4, VA RVSN, Serpukhov, Russia, 2012.

Rukshin, A. S., "Doktrinal'nye vzgliady po voprosam primeneniia i stroitel'stva Vooruzhennykh sil Rossii," *Voennaia mysl'*, No. 3, 2007, pp. 22–28.

"Russia, China Do Not Plan to Create Any Military Union – Russian Presidential Staff Chief," TASS, July 10, 2014.

Russian Defense Policy, "Arctic Interceptors," blog post, January 18, 2021. As of February 5, 2021:
https://russiandefpolicy.com/2021/01/18/arctic-interceptors/

"S-400 Missile System," web page, Wikipedia, last updated July 11, 2021. As of July 13, 2021:
https://en.wikipedia.org/wiki/S-400_missile_system

Saifetdinov, Kh. I., "Aleksandr Andreevich Svechin—vydaiushchiisia voennyi myslitel' nachala XX veka," *Voennaia mysl'*, No. 8, 2018, pp. 101–109.

Savelov, Aleksei, "Chislennost' voennosluzhashchikh po kontraktu v Rossiiskoi armiii vozrosla bolee chem v dva raza," *Tvzvezda.ru*, November 6, 2018.

Serzhantov, A. A., "Tendentsii razvitiia voennogo iskusstva," *Nezavisimoe voennoe obozrenie*, October 4, 2019.

Sivkov, Konstantin, "Kazachestvo kak novyi rod voisk," *Voenno-promyshlennyi kur'er*, March 10, 2014.

Shapiro, Jacob L., "Russia and China's Alliance of Convenience," blog post, *Geopolitical Futures*, December 26, 2017. As of July 16, 2021:
https://geopoliticalfutures.com/russia-chinas-alliance-convenience-1/

Shevtsov, Igor, "Perspektivy razvitiia sukhoputnykh voisk i voenno-morskogo flota VS RF na sovremennom etape," Moscow: Military Training Center of the Ground Forces—Combined Arms Academy of the Armed Forces of the Russian Federation, 2018.

Shifrinson, Joshua, "Russia: A Problem, Not a Threat," *Newsweek*, April 21, 2021.

Shishkin, Aleksandr, "Klassifikatsiia boevykh korablei VMF RF," blog post, LiveJournal, May 23, 2015. As of February 4, 2021: https://navy-korabel.livejournal.com/98354.html

Shlapak, David A., *The Russian Challenge*, Santa Monica, Calif.: RAND Corporation, PE-250-A, 2018. As of July 14, 2021: https://www.rand.org/pubs/perspectives/PE250.html

Shoigu, Sergei, "Armiia Rossii kardinal'no obnovlena," *Krasnaia zvezda*, March 13, 2019.

Shoigu, S. K., "Vystuplenie ministra oborny Rossiiskoi Federatsii generala armii S. K. Shoigu," *Vestnik Akademii voennykh nauk*, Vol. 1, No. 42, 2013, p. 7.

Skarzynski, Stanislaw, and Daniel Wong, "Is Putin's Russia Seeking a New Balance Between China and the West?" *The Diplomat*, August 28, 2020.

Slipchenko, V., "Informatsionnyi resurs i informatsionnoe protivoborstvo," *Armeiskii sbornik*, No. 10, 2013, pp. 52–57.

Smirnov, V. V., "Kontraktnaia armiia v Rossii: problemy i puti ikh reshenii," *Voennaia mysl'*, No. 2, February 2003, pp. 2–7.

Solomentseva, Anastasia, "The 'Rise' of China in the Eyes of Russia: A Source of Threat or New Opportunities?" *Connections*, Vol. 14, No. 1, Winter 2014, pp. 3–40.

State Council Information Office of the People's Republic of China, *China's National Defense in the New Era*, July 24, 2019.

Stent, Angela, "Russia and China: Axis of Revisionists?" Washington, D.C.: Brookings Institution, February 2020.

Stepanov, Aleksandr, "They Have Deployed a Dome, Which Defends from Missiles, over the Russian Bases in Syria. Unique Electronic Warfare Systems, Which Are Capable of 'Blinding' Any Precision-Guided Weapon, Provide It," *MK Online*, interview with Major-General Lastochkin, April 15, 2018.

Stepovoi, Bogdan, Aleksei Ramm, and Evgenii Andreev, "V rezerv po kontraktu," *Izvestiya*, February 13, 2018.

Sterlin, A. E., A. A. Protasov, and S. V. Kreidin, "Sovremennye transformatsii kontseptsii i silovykh instrumentov strategicheskogo sderzhivaniia," *Voennaia mysl'*, No. 8, 2019, pp. 7–17.

Stockholm International Peace Research Institute, "SIPRI Arms Transfers Database," webpage, last updated March 15, 2021. As of July 13, 2021: https://www.sipri.org/databases/armstransfers

Stukalin, Aleksandr, "K voprosu o sovremennom sostoyanii Voenno-transportnoi aviatsii v Rossii," *Eksport vooruzhenii*, Vol. 33, No. 5, September–October 2017, pp. 57–63.

Svechin, Aleksandr A., *Strategy*, Kent D. Lee, ed., Minneapolis, Minn.: East View Publications, 1991.

Surovikin, S. V., and Iu. V. Kuleshov, "Osobennosti organizatsii upravleniia mezhvidovoi gruppirovkoi voisk (sil) v interesakh kompleksnoi bor'by s protivnikom," *Voennaia mysl'*, No. 8, 2017, pp. 5–6.

Tashlykov, S. L., "Obshchie cherty i nekotorye osobennosti soderzhaniia sovremennykh voennykh konfliktov s uchastiem SShA i ikh soiuznikov," *Voennaia mysl'*, No. 8, 2010, pp. 20–28.

Tebin, Prokhor, "O chislennosti Vooruzhennykh sil RF," blog post, LiveJournal, December 12, 2015. As of September 14, 2021: https://prokhor-tebin.livejournal.com/953498.html

Thomas, Timothy, *Kremlin Kontrol: Russia's Political-Military Reality*, Fort Leavenworth, Kan.: Foreign Military Studies Office, 2017.

Thomas, Timothy L., "Russian Forecasts of Future War," *Military Review*, Vol. 99, No. 3, May–June 2019, pp. 84–93.

Thomas, Timothy L., "Information Weapons: Russia's Nonnuclear Strategic Weapon of Choice," *Cyber Defense Review*, Vol. 5, No. 2, Summer 2020, pp. 125–144.

Trenin, Dimitri, *True Partners? How Russia and China See Each Other*, Moscow: Centre for European Reform, Moscow Carnegie Center, 2012.

Trenin, Dmitrii, "Kitai trebuet pristalnogo vnimania," Moscow Carnegie Center Briefing, Vol. 3, No. 5, May 2001.

Trofimov, Yaroslav, and Thomas Grove, "Weary Russia Tries to Avoid Entanglement in US-China Spat," *Wall Street Journal*, June 22, 2020.

Troush, Sergei, *Final Report: Russia's Responses to the NATO Expansion: China Factor*, NATO Democratic Institutions Fellowships 1997–1999, Moscow, 1999.

Tsyrendorzhiev, Sambu, "Prognoz voennykh opasnostei i ugroz Rossii," *Zashchita i bezopasnost'*, Vol. 4, 2015.

Tsygichko, Vitalii, *Models in the System of Strategic Decisions in the USSR*, Lambert Academic Publishing, 2017.

Tsyigichko, V. N., "O kategorii 'sootnoshenie sil' v potentsial'nykh voennykh konfliktakh," *Voennaia mysl'*, No. 2, 2002, pp. 54–63.

U.S.-China Economic and Security Review Commission, "Section 2: An Uneasy Entente: China-Russia Relations in a New Era of Strategic Competition with the United States," in *Report to Congress: U.S. China Economic and Security Review Commission*, Washington, D.C.: U.S. Government Publishing Office, November 2019.

"V VS RF na vsekh strategicheskikh napravleniiakh sozdany samodostatochnye gruppirovki voisk," TASS, November 7, 2017.

"Vesti," *Krasnaia zvezda*, August 2, 2014.

Valdai Discussion Club, "Vladimir Putin Meets with Members of the Valdai Discussion Club," event transcript, webpage, October 18, 2018. As of January 31, 2021:
https://valdaiclub.com/events/posts/articles/
vladimir-putin-meets-with-valdai-discussion-club/

Vadim Volkovitskii, "Prikrytie strategicheskikh iadernykh sil—vazhneishaia zadacha voenno-vozdushnykh sil," *Vozdushno-kosmicheskaia sfera*, No. 6, 2009, pp. 6–19.

Vikulov, S. F., ed., *Aktual'nye problemy realizatsii voenno-ekonomicheskogo potentsiala Rossii v pervoi chetverti XXI veka i osnovnye napravleniia voenno-ekonomicheskikh issledovanii*, Kniga 2, Kantsler, 2019.

Volkov, Sergei, "Voiska PVO nakanune 'raskassatsii'," *Vozdushno-kosmicheskaia sfera*, No. 2, 2006, pp. 10–17.

Waltz, Kenneth N., *Theory of International Politics*, Reading, Mass: Addison-Wesley Publishing Company, 1979.

Weitz, Richard, "Assessing the Sino-Russian Baltic Sea Drill," *China Brief*, Vol. 17, No. 12, September 20, 2017. As of January 10, 2021:
https://jamestown.org/program/assessing-the-sino-russian-baltic-sea-drill/

Weitz, Richard, *Parsing Chinese-Russian Military Exercises*, Carlisle, Pa.: Strategic Studies Institute, U.S. Army War College, 2015.

Westerlund, Fredrik and Susanne Oxenstierna, eds., *Russian Military Capability in a Ten-Year Perspective—2019*, Stockholm: Swedish Defence Research Agency, FOI-R--4758--SE, December 2019.

Xi Jinping, "New Asian Security Concept for New Progress in Security Cooperation," remarks at the Fourth Summit of the Conference on Interaction and Confidence Building Measures in Asia, Shanghai: Shanghai Expo Center, May 21, 2014.

Yeung, Christina, and Nebojsa Bjelakovic, "The Sino-Russian Strategic Partnership: Views from Beijing and Moscow," *Journal of Slavic Military Studies*, Vol. 23, No. 2, 2010, pp. 243–281.

Zagorskii, A. V., "Iadernoe oruzhiia v Evropa: vokrug status-kvo" *Kontury global'noi transformatsii: politika, ekonomika, pravo*, Vol. 11, No. 6, 2018, pp. 128–143.

Zarudnitskii, V. B., "Faktory dostizheniia pobedy v voennykh konfliktakh budushchego," *Voennaia mysl'*, Vol. 8, 2021, pp. 34–47.

Zolotarev, V. A., ed., *Istoriia voennoi strategii Rossii*, Kuchkovo pole, 2000.